Television
Production
Workbook

Television Production Workbook

TWELFTH EDITION

Herbert Zettl

San Francisco State University

:: Cengage

Australia • Brazil • Canada • Mexico • Singapore • United Kingdom • United States

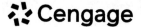

ISBN-13: 978-1-285-46487-9
ISBN-10: 1-285-46487-7

Cengage
200 Pier 4 Boulevard
Boston, MA 02210
USA

Cengage is a leading provider of customized learning solutions with employees residing in nearly 40 different countries and sales in more than 125 countries around the world. Find your local representative at: **www.cengage.com.**

To learn more about Cengage platforms and services, register or access your online learning solution, or purchase materials for your course, visit **www.cengage.com.**

Cover Images: Camera courtesy JVC Professional Products Co.; background © iStockPhoto.com/ AndreasG.

To all the students using this workbook,
which is meant not to reprimand you for what you don't know
but to help you identify what you need to learn

Contents

Preface

This preface is divided into two parts—one for the student and another for the instructor. This should facilitate giving each party specific and relevant information.

FOR THE STUDENT

The *Television Production Workbook* is designed to help you learn the rather complicated subject of television production. The *Workbook* will help you accomplish this task in two ways: by reinforcing what you already know and the information that you have read in the *Television Production Handbook* but also by revealing what you still need to know to become a successful professional member of the television production community and its many branches.

If you could correctly fill in all the bubbles in the *Workbook* without using any outside aids, you would certainly be eligible for an advanced class or a position in a television production company. Even if you think you know the subject pretty well, you may be surprised by the number of questions that give you pause. In fact, finding out what you *don't* know rather than what you do know is often the key to learning and one of the objectives of the *Workbook*. The other objective is, of course, to help you hone your production skills. The features of the *Workbook* are therefore laid out for ease of use and optical learning.

- Each chapter begins with a review of key terms that tests your understanding of the chapter's basic terminology.

- The middle section of each chapter offers a variety of objective questions and production diagrams to analyze. The aim is to help you recognize and apply the production principles discussed in the *Television Production Handbook,* Twelfth Edition.

- A true/false review quiz tests whether you can recall the basic terminology and specific production principles.

- The problem-solving applications at the end of each chapter are intended to enable you to apply to typical production situations the material you have learned. Your instructor will probably come up with many more examples—all in the interest of making the translation from classroom learning to field application maximally efficient and effective.

You will discover that the problems in each chapter differ considerably in degree of difficulty. Some are designed simply for quick recall, others for a more careful weighing of several possible options. Don't get overconfident when you can correctly answer the more obvious questions; you may miss the answers to the more demanding ones. Be aware that some of the problems require the filling in of two or more bubbles. In such a case, the problems that require multiple answers are clearly indicated.

Dealing with a workbook is similar to being involved in extensive preproduction activities: both at first seem somewhat irrelevant or at best time-consuming busywork. This is especially true if you think that learning television production consists primarily of mastering the equipment. But later, when facing production challenges as a professional, you will undoubtedly draw on your rigorous academic problem-solving practice, whether or not you are cognizant of your classroom training.

FOR THE INSTRUCTOR

Because the *Workbook* is primarily an instrument for testing, it is not always embraced by students who may feel that their time is better spent getting outside the classroom, capturing exciting video. Underlying such an attitude is often a justified test-anxiety. To minimize or even eliminate such a mindset, you may try using the *Workbook* as a diagnostic tool, choosing not to grade the results but simply to make students aware of what they have yet to learn. The initial resistance to the *Workbook* quickly dissipates when even the more experienced students realize that they still have some brushing up to do and that your course offers the opportunity to overcome their deficiencies. You could also have students complete part of the *Workbook* problems at the beginning of each classroom period. In any case, you should encourage students to solve the assigned *Workbook* problems at least initially without the aid of the *Handbook*.

The chapters in this edition of the *Workbook* correspond to those of the *Television Production Handbook,* Twelfth Edition, without necessarily being tied to them. You can assign them in the chapter order you use for the *Handbook* or any other order if more convenient or effective.

To expedite scoring the assignments in the *Workbook,* filling in bubbles substitutes for handwritten answers. Although this binary method may confine some students' urge to express themselves creatively, it facilitates speedy evaluation and, more importantly, enables you to compare the standardized scores. The *Instructor's Manual with Answer Key to Workbook,* available online, suggests ways to manage the bubble answers most efficiently.

The problem-solving applications are intended for classroom discussion, but you can also assign them as homework.

If you are using *Zettl's VideoLab 4.0* DVD-ROM, its various modules dovetail smoothly with the *Workbook* exercises. For example, you can use the disc to demonstrate some motion concepts that are impossible to properly show in the main text or the *Workbook,* such as the reversal of motion vectors when crossing the line.

Zettl's VideoLab 4.0 Windows- and Mac-compatible DVD-ROM gives students virtual hands-on practice and a proven shortcut from reading about production techniques to actually applying them in the studio and in the field. The in-text ZVL cues in the *Handbook* refer to *Zettl's VideoLab 4.0.*

Finally, you may want to remind students that they have chosen your class precisely because they want to go beyond simple equipment skills—to move from gifted amateur to creative and responsible professional, from someone who conveniently submits to the industry routines to one who innovates new and more effective ways of communicating significant ideas to media consumers.

To access additional course materials and free companion resources, please visit *www.cengagebrain.com*. At the CengageBrain.com home page, search for the ISBN of the *Television Production Handbook* (978-1-285-05267-0), using the search box at the top of the page. This will take you to the product page, where companion resources can be found.

ACKNOWLEDGMENTS

As usual, the people at Cengage Learning were most cooperative and helpful in the scheduling and preparation of the *Workbook*. My thanks go to Kelli Strieby, product manager; Erin Bosco, associate content developer; and Katie Walsh, product assistant.

I am especially indebted to Gary Palmatier of Ideas and Images, art director and project manager, and Elizabeth von Radics, copy editor, who collaborated on changing the old *Workbook* bubble system so that it aligns more readily with the standard testing format. These two outstanding professionals make a dream team for my work not only because they are at the top of their field but also because they know what video production is all about. Ultimately, the beneficiary of this combination is the media student who gets to work with a maximally effective learning aid.

As with previous editions, I am most grateful to Ed Aiona, expert photographer and artist, and my former colleagues at San Francisco State University Hamid Khani and Chief Engineer Michel French, who were always ready with advice and technical help. I would also like to thank the many students who contributed significantly, however unknowingly, to my formulating the various problems. The ones who doubled as on-camera talent deserve special praise.

Again, I owe a big thank-you to my wife, Erika, who as a longtime classroom teacher, administrator, and educational consultant helped with translating the more complicated problems into a binary format that enables students to give the answers by filling in bubbles.

1 The Television Production Process

REVIEW OF KEY TERMS

Match each term with its appropriate definition by filling in the corresponding bubble.

(A) effect-to-cause model
(B) EFP
(C) postproduction editing
(D) preproduction
(E) medium requirements

(F) television system
(G) postproduction
(H) production
(I) clip
(J) ENG

(K) process message
(L) technical personnel
(M) nontechnical production personnel
(N) multicamera system

1. preparation of all production details

1 Ⓐ Ⓑ Ⓒ Ⓓ Ⓔ
   Ⓕ Ⓖ Ⓗ Ⓘ Ⓙ
   Ⓚ Ⓛ Ⓜ Ⓝ

2. allows random access to, and flexible sequencing of, recorded video and audio material

2 Ⓐ Ⓑ Ⓒ Ⓓ Ⓔ
   Ⓕ Ⓖ Ⓗ Ⓘ Ⓙ
   Ⓚ Ⓛ Ⓜ Ⓝ

3. any production activity that occurs after the production

3 Ⓐ Ⓑ Ⓒ Ⓓ Ⓔ
   Ⓕ Ⓖ Ⓗ Ⓘ Ⓙ
   Ⓚ Ⓛ Ⓜ Ⓝ

PAGE TOTAL [   ]

(A) effect-to-cause model	(F) television system	(K) process message
(B) EFP	(G) postproduction	(L) technical personnel
(C) postproduction editing	(H) production	(M) nontechnical production personnel
(D) preproduction	(I) clip	(N) multicamera system
(E) medium requirements	(J) ENG	

4. the information that the viewer actually receives

4 A B C D E
   F G H I J
   K L M N

5. a brief shot series identified by filename

5 A B C D E
   F G H I J
   K L M N

6. television production that covers daily events and is usually transmitted live or after immediate postproduction

6 A B C D E
   F G H I J
   K L M N

7. the people, content, and production elements needed to generate the desired viewer effect

7 A B C D E
   F G H I J
   K L M N

8. people who primarily operate television equipment

8 A B C D E
   F G H I J
   K L M N

PAGE TOTAL

9. a relatively uncomplicated field production shot for postproduction

9
○ ○ ○ ○ ○
A   B   C   D   E
○ ○ ○ ○ ○
F   G   H   I   J
○ ○ ○ ○
K   L   M   N

10. moving from the idea to the program objective, then backing up to the specific medium requirements to produce this objective

10
○ ○ ○ ○ ○
A   B   C   D   E
○ ○ ○ ○ ○
F   G   H   I   J
○ ○ ○ ○
K   L   M   N

11. the basic equipment necessary to produce video and audio signals and reconvert them into pictures and sound

11
○ ○ ○ ○ ○
A   B   C   D   E
○ ○ ○ ○ ○
F   G   H   I   J
○ ○ ○ ○
K   L   M   N

12. all activities during the recording or televising of an event

12
○ ○ ○ ○ ○
A   B   C   D   E
○ ○ ○ ○ ○
F   G   H   I   J
○ ○ ○ ○
K   L   M   N

13. a production that uses more than one camera

13
○ ○ ○ ○ ○
A   B   C   D   E
○ ○ ○ ○ ○
F   G   H   I   J
○ ○ ○ ○
K   L   M   N

14. production personnel that includes producers and directors

14
○ ○ ○ ○ ○
A   B   C   D   E
○ ○ ○ ○ ○
F   G   H   I   J
○ ○ ○ ○
K   L   M   N

PAGE TOTAL [ ]

SECTION TOTAL [ ]

REVIEW OF EFFECT-TO-CAUSE MODEL

1. Identify each part of the effect-to-cause diagram below and fill in the bubbles with the corresponding letters.

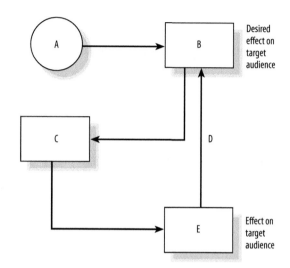

a. program content, people, and production elements

b. feedback

c. defined process message

d. actual process message

e. initial idea

1a ⭕ ⭕ ⭕ ⭕ ⭕
    A B C D E

1b ⭕ ⭕ ⭕ ⭕ ⭕
    A B C D E

1c ⭕ ⭕ ⭕ ⭕ ⭕
    A B C D E

1d ⭕ ⭕ ⭕ ⭕ ⭕
    A B C D E

1e ⭕ ⭕ ⭕ ⭕ ⭕
    A B C D E

P A G E
T O T A L

Select the correct answers and fill in the bubbles with the corresponding letters.

2. The effect-to-cause model is especially helpful in (A) *preproduction* (B) *production* (C) *postproduction.*

   2 ○ A   ○ B   ○ C

3. Medium requirements are basically determined by the (A) *chief engineer* (B) *available equipment* (C) *defined process message.*

   3 ○ A   ○ B   ○ C

4. Feedback helps determine (A) *whether the production was efficient* (B) *how close the actual effect came to the defined process message* (C) *how close the actual effect came to the original idea.*

   4 ○ A   ○ B   ○ C

5. The most important initial step in the effect-to-cause approach is (A) *determining the medium requirements* (B) *determining the available production equipment* (C) *defining the process message.*

   5 ○ A   ○ B   ○ C

6. In the effect-to-cause model, we move from (A) *idea to medium requirements to production* (B) *idea to production to process message* (C) *idea to process message to medium requirements.*

   6 ○ A   ○ B   ○ C

7. The angle will define the (A) *process message* (B) *basic production approach* (C) *position of the camera.*

   7 ○ A   ○ B   ○ C

8. A defined process message must contain at least the (A) *target audience* (B) *medium requirements* (C) *desired effect on the viewer.*

   8 ○ A   ○ B   ○ C

9. The effect-to-cause model is especially useful in the production of (A) *breaking news stories* (B) *documentaries* (C) *dramas.*

   9 ○ A   ○ B   ○ C

10. The medium requirements include (A) *equipment and people* (B) *equipment but not people* (C) *people but not equipment.*

    10 ○ A   ○ B   ○ C

PAGE TOTAL [   ]

SECTION TOTAL [   ]

REVIEW OF PRODUCTION PERSONNEL

1. Match each job title with the most appropriate function by filling in the corresponding bubble.

(A) director   (E) VR operator   (H) floor manager
(B) PA   (F) LD   (I) DP
(C) AD   (G) producer   (J) TD
(D) floor person

a. relays the director's messages to talent

1a ( )A ( )B ( )C ( )D ( )E
    ( )F ( )G ( )H ( )I ( )J

b. supports the director in directing activities

1b ( )A ( )B ( )C ( )D ( )E
    ( )F ( )G ( )H ( )I ( )J

c. in charge of video-recording

1c ( )A ( )B ( )C ( )D ( )E
    ( )F ( )G ( )H ( )I ( )J

d. in EFP, works the camera; in cinema, is in charge of the lighting and film exposure

1d ( )A ( )B ( )C ( )D ( )E
    ( )F ( )G ( )H ( )I ( )J

e. in charge of lighting

1e ( )A ( )B ( )C ( )D ( )E
    ( )F ( )G ( )H ( )I ( )J

f. in charge of all preproduction activities

1f ( )A ( )B ( )C ( )D ( )E
    ( )F ( )G ( )H ( )I ( )J

g. in charge of all production activities on the production day

1g ( )A ( )B ( )C ( )D ( )E
    ( )F ( )G ( )H ( )I ( )J

PAGE TOTAL [   ]

h. assists producer and director in all production phases

A B C D E
F G H I J

i. in charge of a crew; usually does the switching

1i A B C D E
F G H I J

j. operates cue cards

1j A B C D E
F G H I J

2. Match each title of news personnel with its appropriate definition by filling in the corresponding bubble.

(A) writer   (D) news director   (G) videographer/shooter
(B) sportscaster   (E) reporter   (H) anchor
(C) news producer   (F) assignment editor   (I) VJ

a. on-camera talent, giving sports content

2a A B C D E
F G H I

b. principal presenter of newscast, normally from a studio set

2b A B C D E
F G H I

c. operates camcorder and, in the absence of a reporter, decides what part of the event to cover

2c A B C D E
F G H I

d. responsible for the selection and the placement of the stories in a newscast

2d A B C D E
F G H I

e. prepares on-the-air copy for the anchorpersons

2e A B C D E
F G H I

PAGE TOTAL [   ]

(A)	writer	(D)	news director	(G)	videographer/shooter
(B)	sportscaster	(E)	reporter	(H)	anchor
(C)	news producer	(F)	assignment editor	(I)	VJ

f. combines in a single person the camera operator, the editor, the writer, and sometimes even the on-camera talent in news gathering

2f ○ ○ ○ ○ ○
    A B C D E
    ○ ○ ○ ○
    F G H I

g. gathers the news stories and often reports on-camera from the field

2g ○ ○ ○ ○ ○
    A B C D E
    ○ ○ ○ ○
    F G H I

h. sends reporters and videographers to specific events

2h ○ ○ ○ ○ ○
    A B C D E
    ○ ○ ○ ○
    F G H I

i. in charge of all the news operations

2i ○ ○ ○ ○ ○
    A B C D E
    ○ ○ ○ ○
    F G H I

PAGE TOTAL

SECTION TOTAL

REVIEW OF TECHNICAL SYSTEMS

1. Identify each of the major elements of the basic television system by filling in the corresponding bubble.

   a. video signal   **d.** VR   **f.** audio signal

   b. loudspeaker   **e.** TV camera   **g.** transmission

   c. microphone

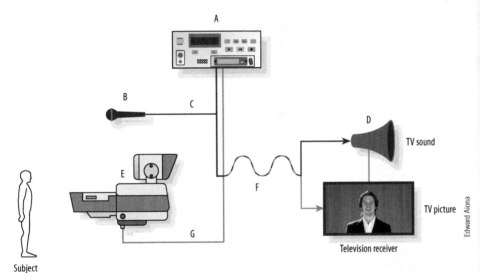

1a ○ ○ ○ ○
    A B C D
    ○ ○ ○
    E F G

1b ○ ○ ○ ○
    A B C D
    ○ ○ ○
    E F G

1c ○ ○ ○ ○
    A B C D
    ○ ○ ○
    E F G

1d ○ ○ ○ ○
    A B C D
    ○ ○ ○
    E F G

1e ○ ○ ○ ○
    A B C D
    ○ ○ ○
    E F G

1f ○ ○ ○ ○
    A B C D
    ○ ○ ○
    E F G

1g ○ ○ ○ ○
    A B C D
    ○ ○ ○
    E F G

P A G E
T O T A L

2. Identify each major component of the multicamera studio system by filling in the corresponding bubble.

a. CCUs 1 and 2

b. cameras 1 and 2

c. home TV receiver

d. preview monitors

e. line monitor

f. video switcher

g. video recorder

h. audio console

i. transmitter

j. audio monitor (speaker)

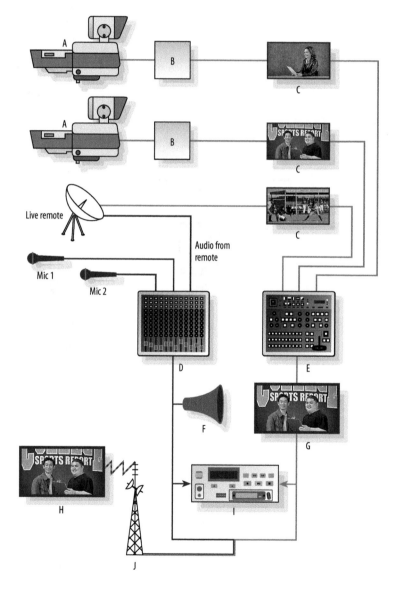

Live remote

Audio from remote

Mic 1

Mic 2

A

B

C

D

E

F

G

H

I

J

2a ○ ○ ○ ○ ○
    A B C D E
    ○ ○ ○ ○ ○
    F G H I J

2b ○ ○ ○ ○ ○
    A B C D E
    ○ ○ ○ ○ ○
    F G H I J

2c ○ ○ ○ ○ ○
    A B C D E
    ○ ○ ○ ○ ○
    F G H I J

2d ○ ○ ○ ○ ○
    A B C D E
    ○ ○ ○ ○ ○
    F G H I J

2e ○ ○ ○ ○ ○
    A B C D E
    ○ ○ ○ ○ ○
    F G H I J

2f ○ ○ ○ ○ ○
    A B C D E
    ○ ○ ○ ○ ○
    F G H I J

2g ○ ○ ○ ○ ○
    A B C D E
    ○ ○ ○ ○ ○
    F G H I J

2h ○ ○ ○ ○ ○
    A B C D E
    ○ ○ ○ ○ ○
    F G H I J

2i ○ ○ ○ ○ ○
    A B C D E
    ○ ○ ○ ○ ○
    F G H I J

2j ○ ○ ○ ○ ○
    A B C D E
    ○ ○ ○ ○ ○
    F G H I J

P A G E
T O T A L

Edward Aiona

3. Match each system element with its appropriate function by filling in the corresponding bubble.

(A) cameras
(B) preview monitors
(C) TV receiver
(D) audio monitor (speaker)
(E) line monitor

(F) microphones
(G) switcher
(H) audio console
(I) CCUs
(J) VR

a. selects video inputs

3a ○ ○ ○ ○ ○
    A B C D E
    ○ ○ ○ ○ ○
    F G H I J

b. translates the broadcast signals into pictures and sound

3b ○ ○ ○ ○ ○
    A B C D E
    ○ ○ ○ ○ ○
    F G H I J

c. controls the picture quality of the television cameras

3c ○ ○ ○ ○ ○
    A B C D E
    ○ ○ ○ ○ ○
    F G H I J

d. converts what we hear into electrical signals

3d ○ ○ ○ ○ ○
    A B C D E
    ○ ○ ○ ○ ○
    F G H I J

e. converts what the lens sees into electrical signals

3e ○ ○ ○ ○ ○
    A B C D E
    ○ ○ ○ ○ ○
    F G H I J

f. controls the audio quality of the various audio inputs

3f ○ ○ ○ ○ ○
    A B C D E
    ○ ○ ○ ○ ○
    F G H I J

g. records video and audio signals on recording media

3g ○ ○ ○ ○ ○
    A B C D E
    ○ ○ ○ ○ ○
    F G H I J

P A G E
T O T A L [   ]

(A) cameras	(F) microphones
(B) preview monitors	(G) switcher
(C) TV receiver	(H) audio console
(D) audio monitor (speaker)	(I) CCUs
(E) line monitor	(J) VR

h. reproduces the line-out sound

3h ○ ○ ○ ○ ○
    A B C D E
    ○ ○ ○ ○ ○
    F G H I J

i. displays the line-out pictures

3i ○ ○ ○ ○ ○
    A B C D E
    ○ ○ ○ ○ ○
    F G H I J

j. displays the pictures supplied by the various video sources

3j ○ ○ ○ ○ ○
    A B C D E
    ○ ○ ○ ○ ○
    F G H I J

PAGE TOTAL [ ]

SECTION TOTAL [ ]

REVIEW QUIZ

*Mark the following statements as true or false by filling in the bubbles in the **T** (for true) or **F** (for false) column.*

		T	F
1.	A microphone converts digital sound into analog signals.	1 ◯	◯
2.	A camcorder can use memory cards to record video and audio inputs.	2 ◯	◯
3.	In a television studio, we use spotlights and floodlights.	3 ◯	◯
4.	A video switcher can select incoming sources but cannot perform transitions.	4 ◯	◯
5.	All audio consoles can select the signals from incoming audio sources and control sound volume.	5 ◯	◯
6.	The effect-to-cause model recommends moving directly from basic show idea to the necessary production equipment.	6 ◯	◯
7.	The process message refers to the director's effective communication of the production process to the technical personnel.	7 ◯	◯
8.	The medium requirements are greatly influenced by the defined process message.	8 ◯	◯
9.	*Postproduction editing* refers to starting with the end of the show and working your way toward the beginning with your editing sequence.	9 ◯	◯
10.	In the news department, a VJ is an intern who does various jobs.	10 ◯	◯

SECTION
TOTAL [   ]

PROBLEM-SOLVING APPLICATIONS

Think through each production problem and consider the various options. Then pick the most effective solution and justify your choice.

1. List in any order the major components (equipment) of the multicamera studio system that will allow you to produce and select optimal pictures from three cameras, produce optimal sound from four microphones, and video-record and simultaneously transmit the signals to a television receiver. Now order these components and connect them with lines that show the basic signal flow from cameras, microphones, and the various video and audio controls to the video recorder and the home television receiver.

2. The program manager asks you, the producer, to come up with an equipment list for a show on water conservation. What additional information do you need?

3. What system elements are incorporated into a single camcorder? What are some of the advantages and the disadvantages of the camcorder system compared with those of the multicamera studio system?

4. What exactly distinguishes ENG from EFP?

5. Apply the effect-to-cause model to a variety of goal-directed programs. Pay particular attention to a precise process message.

6. How does a clearly defined process message help with the medium requirements?

7. List two tapeless digital recording media and describe the advantages and the disadvantages of each.

2 The Producer in Preproduction

REVIEW OF KEY TERMS

Match each term with its appropriate definition by filling in the corresponding bubble.

(A) rating   (D) program proposal   (G) time line
(B) demographics   (E) production schedule   (H) target audience
(C) share   (F) treatment   (I) psychographics

1. a breakdown of time blocks for various activities on the actual production day

2. audience factors concerned with such data as consumer buying habits, values, and lifestyles

3. percentage of television households tuned to a specific station in relation to all HUT

4. percentage of television households tuned to a specific station in relation to the total number of television households

PAGE TOTAL

(A) rating	(D) program proposal	(G) time line
(B) demographics	(E) production schedule	(H) target audience
(C) share	(F) treatment	(I) psychographics

5. the calendar dates for preproduction, production, and postproduction activities

5 ○ ○ ○ ○ ○
  A B C D E
  ○ ○ ○ ○
  F G H I

6. written document that outlines the program objective and the major aspects of a television presentation

6 ○ ○ ○ ○ ○
  A B C D E
  ○ ○ ○ ○
  F G H I

7. audience factors concerned with such data as age, gender, marital status, and income

7 ○ ○ ○ ○ ○
  A B C D E
  ○ ○ ○ ○
  F G H I

8. narrative description of a television program

8 ○ ○ ○ ○ ○
  A B C D E
  ○ ○ ○ ○
  F G H I

9. viewers identified to receive a specific message

9 ○ ○ ○ ○ ○
  A B C D E
  ○ ○ ○ ○
  F G H I

PAGE TOTAL

SECTION TOTAL

REVIEW OF PREPRODUCTION PLANNING: GENERATING IDEAS

1. Expand three of the following four clusters according to the key word. Develop a precise process message for each. Choose the key word for the fourth cluster and define its process message accordingly.

   a. cluster 1

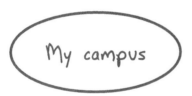

   Defined process message: _____

   _____

   _____

   _____

   _____

   _____

b. cluster 2

Tolerance

Defined process message: _____

_____

_____

_____

_____

_____

c. cluster 3

Friendship

Defined process message: _____

_____

_____

_____

_____

_____

d. cluster 4 (on a subject of your choice)

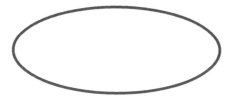

Defined process message: _____

_____

_____

_____

_____

_____

Course No. _____   Date _____   Name _____

REVIEW OF EVALUATING IDEAS

Select the correct answers and fill in the bubbles with the corresponding letters.

1. In the preproduction flowchart below, match the unmarked steps with the corresponding letters.

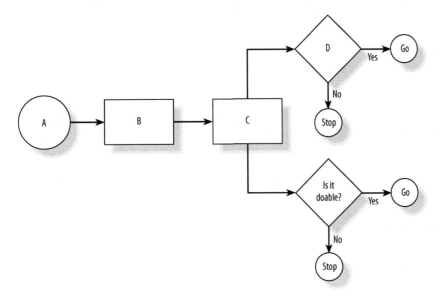

a. angle

b. idea

c. Is it worth doing?

d. process message

1a ⭕ ⭕ ⭕ ⭕
    A B C D

1b ⭕ ⭕ ⭕ ⭕
    A B C D

1c ⭕ ⭕ ⭕ ⭕
    A B C D

1d ⭕ ⭕ ⭕ ⭕
    A B C D

SECTION TOTAL

REVIEW OF PROGRAM PROPOSAL

Select the correct answers and fill in the bubbles with the corresponding letters.

1. Preproduction is necessary for (A) *every production except ENG* (B) *studio productions only* (C) *EFPs only.*

   1 ○ A ○ B ○ C

2. In a large production, the daily activities are supervised by the (A) *PA* (B) *executive producer* (C) *line producer.*

   2 ○ A ○ B ○ C

3. A defined process message should (A) *include the specific objective of the show* (B) *state the steps of moving from idea to finished show* (C) *describe the process of moving from idea to detailed script.*

   3 ○ A ○ B ○ C

4. A good description of the target audience should include (A) *only demographic indicators* (B) *the number of potential viewers* (C) *demographic and psychographic indicators.*

   4 ○ A ○ B ○ C

5. When preparing a budget for an outside client, you can skip the cost for (A) *the writer* (B) *the equipment* (C) *neither the writer nor the equipment.*

   5 ○ A ○ B ○ C

6. A show treatment usually contains a (A) *brief narrative description of what the audience will see and hear* (B) *script sample with major visualization cues* (C) *one-page sample of the dialogue and the video and audio cues.*

   6 ○ A ○ B ○ C

7. The standard program proposal usually contains a (A) *program objective* (B) *list of studio or remote equipment* (C) *detailed storyboard.*

   7 ○ A ○ B ○ C

8. The individual who is normally not needed during the early stage of preproduction is the (A) *director* (B) *chief engineer* (C) *producer.*

   8 ○ A ○ B ○ C

9. In the production schedule on the facing page, identify potential problems for each EFP shoot. From the list below, select the items that best describe the problems and fill in the corresponding bubbles. Most shoots have more than one problem. *(Multiple answers are possible.)*

   (A) different talent; break in continuity

   (B) different director and crew; potential break in style and continuity

   (C) need for remote truck questionable relative to the production scope

   (D) shooting time too late; will cause lighting and continuity problems in postproduction

   (E) should be done in conjunction with similar previous activity or opening

   (F) facilities request very late

   (G) facilities request too late

   (H) too little time allotted

   (I) too much time allotted

PAGE TOTAL [   ]

Show/Scene/Subject	Date/Time	Location	Facilities	Talent/Personnel
Leisure City SHOOT 1 OPENING	Aug. 8 8:30 am 4:30 pm	In front of completed model home— Simple opening remarks. 1:00 min.	Normal EFP as per fac. req. Aug. 8	Talent: LYNNE Director: B.R. Crew A scheduled
Leisure City SHOOT 2	Aug. 9 12:30 pm 1:00 pm	Homes under construction. Show homes being constructed.	Special remote Truck. See equipment fac. req. Aug. 8	Talent: LYNNE Director: B.R. Crew A scheduled
Leisure City SHOOT 3	Aug. 10 8:30 am 9:00 am	Interior of model home. Show show Typical home looks and works inside.	Normal EFP as per fac. req. Aug. 7	Talent: LYNNE Director: B.R. Crew A scheduled
Leisure City SHOOT 4	Aug. 11 7:30 pm 10:30 pm	Homes under construction.	Normal EFP as per fac. req. Aug. 11	Talent: SUSAN Director: JOHN HEWITT Crew B scheduled
Leisure City SHOOT 5	Aug. 12 8:00 pm 8:30 pm	In front of completed model home— Simple closing remarks. 1:30 min.	Special remote Truck. See equipment fac. req. Aug. 8	Talent: SUSAN Director: B.R. Crew A scheduled

a. shoot 1

b. shoot 2

c. shoot 3

d. shoot 4

e. shoot 5

9a ○ A ○ B ○ C ○ D ○ E
○ F ○ G ○ H ○ I

9b ○ A ○ B ○ C ○ D ○ E
○ F ○ G ○ H ○ I

9c ○ A ○ B ○ C ○ D ○ E
○ F ○ G ○ H ○ I

9d ○ A ○ B ○ C ○ D ○ E
○ F ○ G ○ H ○ I

9e ○ A ○ B ○ C ○ D ○ E
○ F ○ G ○ H ○ I

PAGE TOTAL [   ]

SECTION TOTAL [   ]

REVIEW OF COORDINATION

Select the correct answers and fill in the bubbles with the corresponding letters.

1. The person principally responsible for all preproduction communication is the (A) *producer* (B) *director* (C) *executive producer.*

    1 ◯ A   ◯ B   ◯ C

2. When coordinating an EFP on water conservation, you need to include in your preproduction memos the (A) *writer* (B) *chief engineer* (C) *sales manager.*

    2 ◯ A   ◯ B   ◯ C

3. In a typical television station, facilities requests are necessary (A) *for every production except ENG* (B) *only if you are planning a new production* (C) *for the preproduction conference.*

    3 ◯ A   ◯ B   ◯ C

4. Informing the crew of the defined process message is the responsibility of the (A) *director* (B) *executive producer* (C) *chief engineer.*

    4 ◯ A   ◯ B   ◯ C

5. The production schedule is usually drawn up by the (A) *executive producer* (B) *producer* (C) *assistant director.*

    5 ◯ A   ◯ B   ◯ C

6. A schedule change is normally communicated to the production team by the (A) *producer* (B) *executive producer* (C) *floor manager.*

    6 ◯ A   ◯ B   ◯ C

7. When sending your memos via e-mail, you must insist on a written response from (A) *production people only* (B) *technical personnel only* (C) *every person on your mailing list.*

    7 ◯ A   ◯ B   ◯ C

SECTION TOTAL

REVIEW OF UNIONS AND LEGAL MATTERS

Select the correct answers and fill in the bubbles with the corresponding letters.

1. A potential sponsor would like a treatment of one of the proposed segments of your humanities series. Sending the script instead is (A) *acceptable* (B) *not acceptable.*

   1 ◯ A   ◯ B

2. The theater department of the local high school would like to play its video production of Arthur Miller's *Death of a Salesman* on a local TV station. The student actors (A) *will* (B) *will not* need SAG-AFTRA clearance.

   2 ◯ A   ◯ B

3. For each of the trade unions listed, mark whether it is a (A) *technical* or a (B) *nontechnical* union by filling in the appropriate bubble.

   a. WGA

   3a ◯ A   ◯ B

   b. IBEW

   3b ◯ A   ◯ B

   c. SEG

   3c ◯ A   ◯ B

   d. NABET

   3d ◯ A   ◯ B

   e. DGA

   3e ◯ A   ◯ B

   f. AFM

   3f ◯ A   ◯ B

   g. IATSE

   3g ◯ A   ◯ B

   h. SAG-AFTRA

   3h ◯ A   ◯ B

PAGE TOTAL [   ]

4. Determine whether each of the production cases below (A) *requires* or (B) *does not require* copyright clearance and fill in the appropriate bubble.

a. using a recent CD recording of Bach's *Toccata and Fugue in F Major* as the theme for a show on architecture

    4a ○ A   ○ B

b. using a Beatles song as the theme for a documentary on the history of rock music

    4b ○ A   ○ B

c. taking close-ups of paintings in your news coverage of the local outdoor art festival

    4c ○ A   ○ B

d. using a sixteenth-century book to make a digital scan of a church floor plan for your Renaissance show

    4d ○ A   ○ B

e. quoting one sentence from a recently published art book

    4e ○ A   ○ B

f. using a record album cover as the background for your opening and closing titles on a music series

    4f ○ A   ○ B

g. using three different scenes of published plays as the basis for your series about acting for the video camera

    4g ○ A   ○ B

h. having your pianist friend play and record her own composition for use as a theme on your weekly music series

    4h ○ A   ○ B

PAGE TOTAL

SECTION TOTAL

REVIEW OF RATINGS

Select the correct answers and fill in the bubbles with the corresponding letters.

1. A rating of 13 indicates that (A) *13 of 2,000* (B) *800 of 6,000* (C) *13 of 1,300*
   (D) *total television households* (E) *of all households using television* are tuned to your
   station. *(Fill in two bubbles.)*

2. Share figures are usually (A) *higher* (B) *lower* than rating figures.

3. A share of 22 means that (A) *175 of 2,200* (B) *22 of 2,200* (C) *175 of 800* (D) *total television
   households* (E) *of all households using television* are tuned to your station.
   (Fill in two bubbles.)

4. All rating services use (A) *audience samples* (B) *total populations* as a basis for
   their figures.

5. HUT is a factor in figuring (A) *shares* (B) *ratings*.

1 ○ ○ ○
   A   B   C
  ○ ○
  D E

2 ○ ○
   A   B

3 ○ ○ ○
   A   B   C
  ○ ○
  D E

4 ○ ○
   A   B

5 ○ ○
   A   B

SECTION TOTAL [ ]

*Mark the following statements as true or false by filling in the bubbles in the **T** (for true) or **F** (for false) column.*

		T	F

1. Normally, it is the writer who establishes the initial production process.   **1** ○ ○

2. A show treatment is necessary only for television documentaries.   **2** ○ ○

3. The two major criteria for evaluating program ideas are *Is it doable?* and *How much does it cost?*   **3** ○ ○

4. The facilities request for a specific production should contain equipment and technical facilities.   **4** ○ ○

5. The line producer is responsible primarily for budgets.   **5** ○ ○

6. Two of the important items in an effective program proposal are a treatment and a description of the target audience.   **6** ○ ○

7. The producer works only with nontechnical personnel.   **7** ○ ○

8. Broadcast unions include technical personnel only.   **8** ○ ○

9. Demographic descriptors help define the target audience.   **9** ○ ○

10. Once you have generated a worthwhile message, the producer can leave the day-to-day production details to the PA.   **10** ○ ○

11. Whereas the budget is essential for a program proposal, a description of the target audience is not.   **11** ○ ○

12. Because production is primarily a creative activity, any type of production system would prove counterproductive.   **12** ○ ○

13. CDs sold in record stores are in the public domain, so you can use them for television productions without securing copyright clearance.   **13** ○ ○

14. A time line and a production schedule are the same thing.   **14** ○ ○

15. Budgets must include expenses for preproduction, production, and all postproduction activities as well as personnel.   **15** ○ ○

SECTION TOTAL [ ]

PROBLEM-SOLVING APPLICATIONS

1. The art director asks you, the producer, whether her floor plan will allow optimal camera traffic. Are you the right person to answer this question? If so, why? If not, who would be the appropriate person to answer this question?

2. Your new comedy series is shot multicamera-style in the studio. You intend to video-record the dress rehearsal and the uninterrupted live-recorded show for later on-air scheduling. The production manager suggests that you prepare a budget that includes a generous amount of money for postproduction editing. Do you agree with the production manager? If so, why? If not, why not?

3. Write an effective program proposal for one or more of the following ideas. The proposal should include these points: (1) program title, (2) target audience, (3) defined process message, (4) show treatment, (5) ideal program time and broadcast or other distribution channel, and (6) tentative budget.

    a. a series of shows about the effects of television violence on children

    b. a weekly fashion show

    c. a 10-week series about how to conserve water

    d. a three-show series about your favorite sport

    e. a five-show series for seventh- and eighth-graders about the dangers of drugs

    f. a 10-part series about human dignity and happiness

    g. a 5-part mini-documentary series about road rage and safe driving

    h. a 10-part series about the various methods of conflict resolution

    i. a 10-part series about the life and the work of your favorite sports figure

4. The local high-school video club has produced a music video, using magazine pictures that are synchronized with the latest recording of a rock band. The students plead with you to persuade the local cable company to put it on the air. What concerns, if any, do you have about airing this video recording? What can you do to accommodate the students' request?

5. The art director claims that she never received the director's e-mail about a set for the upcoming studio show of a dance recital. What simple steps would you suggest to remedy such problems?

3 The Script

REVIEW OF KEY TERMS

Match each term with its appropriate definition by filling in the corresponding bubble.

(A) partial two-column A/V format

(B) event order

(C) goal-directed information

(D) two-column A/V script

(E) classical dramaturgy

(F) show format

(G) single-column drama script

(H) fact sheet

1. traditional script with audio information in the right column and video information in the left

1 Ⓐ Ⓑ Ⓒ Ⓓ
   A B C D
   Ⓔ Ⓕ Ⓖ Ⓗ
   E F G H

2. used to describe a show for which the dialogue is indicated but not completely written out

2 Ⓐ Ⓑ Ⓒ Ⓓ
   A B C D
   Ⓔ Ⓕ Ⓖ Ⓗ
   E F G H

3. the lineup of event details

3 Ⓐ Ⓑ Ⓒ Ⓓ
   A B C D
   Ⓔ Ⓕ Ⓖ Ⓗ
   E F G H

4. a list of routine show segments

4 Ⓐ Ⓑ Ⓒ Ⓓ
   A B C D
   Ⓔ Ⓕ Ⓖ Ⓗ
   E F G H

PAGE TOTAL _____

(A) partial two-column A/V format	(D) two-column A/V script	(G) single-column drama script
(B) event order	(E) classical dramaturgy	(H) fact sheet
(C) goal-directed information	(F) show format	

5. program content intended to be learned by the viewer

5   ○ ○ ○ ○
    A B C D
    ○ ○ ○ ○
    E F G H

6. the technique of dramatic composition

6   ○ ○ ○ ○
    A B C D
    ○ ○ ○ ○
    E F G H

7. lists the items to be shown on-camera and their main features

7   ○ ○ ○ ○
    A B C D
    ○ ○ ○ ○
    E F G H

8. traditional format for dramatic television and motion picture scripts

8   ○ ○ ○ ○
    A B C D
    ○ ○ ○ ○
    E F G H

P A G E
T O T A L [   ]

SECTION
TOTAL   [   ]

Course No. _____ Date _____ Name _____

REVIEW OF BASIC SCRIPT FORMATS

Select the correct answers and fill in the bubbles with the corresponding letters.

1. Each of the following three figures (**a** through **c**) shows a script segment that contains some format errors. For each figure identify the specific format errors: (A) *unnecessary talent instructions* (B) *video or audio instructions in the wrong column* (C) *incomplete dialogue* (D) *unnecessary camera instructions* (E) *nonessential and confusing information.* ***(Multiple answers are possible.)***

a. fully scripted serial drama (excerpt only)

1a ○ ○ ○ ○ ○
    A B C D E

```
GARY'S OFFICE: DAY

GARY is working intensely at his computer and ignores two
telephone calls, when KIM bursts cheerfully into his office.

CUT TO CAMERA 3 WHEN KIM ENTERS

                        KIM

            Let's go for coffee.

         GARY (not looking up)

            Don't have time.

                        KIM

         Oh, shucks, make time.

                       GARY

      You seem to be in a good mood today.

                        KIM

         I'm always in a good mood...

                       GARY

    [Says something about having to finish the report]

                        KIM

    [Tries to persuade GARY to pay more attention to her]

    CUE GARY TO STAND UP AND CUT TO CAMERA 1 WHEN HE GETS UP
```

PAGE
TOTAL   [   ]

b. two-column A/V script of brief feature story on the value of books (excerpt only)

Agency	Hot Stuff	Writer	Mary Smart
Client	Papermill Creek Publishing	Producer	Maurice Smart
Project	Book Promotion	Director	Chul Heo
Title	Books Are Alive!	Art Director	Buzz Palmer
Subject		Medium	EFP HDTV
Job #	011	Contact	Smart
Code #	HZWB11	Draft	2

VIDEO	AUDIO
CU of Becky Take camera 3	BECKY: No, books are certainly not dead. On the contrary, 20 percent more books were printed worldwide last year than in any previous year.
Fade in sound of printing presses	Cue Becky to go to bookcase and look at some books.
CU of Peter. Must look annoyed.	PETER: [Says something about digital storage being so much better than clumsy books.]
Sound of books being dropped	BECKY: CU of her dropping books. Well, I think you are an ignorant nerd. How many books do you own? PETER: None!
Sound of Becky laughing	

c. fact sheet

SHOW: Tech News
DATE: Aug. 20
HOST: Larry W.
PROPS: New Extreme Printer (operational)

1. New super color laser printer.

2. Medium shot of open printer. Zoom in on ink
cartridges. Prints are permanent. Will outlast Grandma's
chemical photos.

3. Pan right to operating panel. Easy, intuitive
operation. Just follow the instructions.

4. CU of operation manual.

5. CU of Larry:

LARRY: Let's do some printing right now and see how easy
it is.

[Larry accesses the printer wirelessly via his laptop.]

LARRY [looks enthusiastic]: As you can see, all I needed
to do is access the picture on my laptop and click the
Print command.

6. And it is quiet. [Larry cups his ears.]

7. Extreme close-up of Larry.

LARRY: Be sure to take advantage of our introductory
offer. But hurry! This once-in-a-lifetime opportunity
expires on Thursday.

GO TO BLACK

PAGE
TOTAL

SECTION
TOTAL

REVIEW OF STORY STRUCTURE, CONFLICT, AND DRAMATURGY

Select the correct answers and fill in the bubbles with the corresponding letters.

1. Select the most common four elements of the basic dramatic story structure: (A) *theme, plot, story, characters* (B) *theme, plot, characters, environment* (C) *plot, characters, action, environment.*

   1 ○ ○ ○
   A B C

2. Read the following very brief treatment excerpts and indicate whether the conflicts are (A) *plot-based* or (B) *character-based.*

   a. A drunk driver goes through a stoplight and hits a car in the intersection. By chance both drivers end up in the same emergency room. They begin discussing the physical danger of driving under the influence. The discussion turns into an argument. One of the drivers crawls out of bed and tries to hit the other one. The nurse stops the fight just in time.

   2a ○ ○
   A B

   b. A young doctor, who has been fascinated with Africa since elementary school, decides to switch from being a successful family care provider to an AIDS researcher at a San Francisco clinic. She finally can't bear the slow progress in the lab any longer and decides to make her first Africa trip to help stem the AIDS epidemic in Zwamumbu [fictitious name]. With the help of an international relief organization, she opens a clinic and, within a short time, has gained the respect and the love of hundreds of adults and children for the "miracles" she performs as a doctor. But during a political uprising of a neighboring warlord, the clinic is invaded and she is accidentally shot in the crossfire.

   2b ○ ○
   A B

   c. A young doctor is summoned by a world health organization to deliver AIDS medicine to a Zwamumbu international health clinic. This is a high-risk mission because the president of Zwamumbu has prohibited any use of AIDS medication. His justification is one of denial. In his words: "We do not have AIDS in our country." After several scary moments, such as the search at airport customs, the doctor not only manages to deliver the medicine but also helps administer it to the children who are already HIV infected. The president's secret service people learn about her activity and get permission to assassinate her. Despite tight security at the clinic, the order is carried out successfully. Posing as an AIDS patient, the assassin confronts the young doctor and, repeating the president's statement, shoots her.

   2c ○ ○
   A B

PAGE
TOTAL [   ]

3. Fill in the bubbles whose letters correspond with the letters in the diagram below, identifying the various principal developmental steps of a classical dramaturgy.

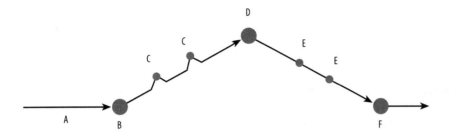

a. falling action and consequences of major crisis

b. exposition

c. resolution

d. point of attack

e. climax

f. rising action and additional conflicts

3a ○ A ○ B ○ C
○ D ○ E ○ F

3b ○ A ○ B ○ C
○ D ○ E ○ F

3c ○ A ○ B ○ C
○ D ○ E ○ F

3d ○ A ○ B ○ C
○ D ○ E ○ F

3e ○ A ○ B ○ C
○ D ○ E ○ F

3f ○ A ○ B ○ C
○ D ○ E ○ F

PAGE
TOTAL

SECTION
TOTAL

REVIEW QUIZ

*Mark the following statements as true or false by filling in the bubbles in the **T** (for true) or **F** (for false) column.*

		T	F
1.	The standard two-column A/V script shows the video information on the left side and the audio information on the right.	1 ○	○
2.	The script is an effective communication device for all three production phases.	2 ○	○
3.	The defined process message is especially useful for programs that contain primarily goal-directed information.	3 ○	○
4.	The rising as well as the falling action can include a number of crises.	4 ○	○
5.	A plot can develop from outside-in or from inside-out.	5 ○	○
6.	The from-outside-in plots are primarily character-based.	6 ○	○
7.	In a classical dramaturgy, the point of attack marks the first major crisis.	7 ○	○
8.	The difference between a standard two-column A/V script and a partial two-column A/V script is that the latter contains no video information.	8 ○	○
9.	In a goal-directed program, the basic idea should lead to a defined process message.	9 ○	○
10.	The fact sheet and the show format have identical script formats.	10 ○	○

SECTION TOTAL [ ]

PROBLEM-SOLVING APPLICATIONS

1. Analyze three or four programs of a dramatic crime series and see whether the conflicts are primarily character-based, plot-based, or both. Justify your analyses.

2. How can you use plot to develop character?

3. Write a treatment of a one-hour special that includes all six elements of the classical dramaturgy.

4. Analyze a single program of a dramatic or comedy series and list all situations (verbal or action) that create an obvious conflict.

4 The Director in Preproduction

REVIEW OF KEY TERMS

Match each term with its appropriate definition by filling in the corresponding bubble.

(A) time line
(B) location sketch
(C) facilities request
(D) locking-in

(E) sequencing
(F) floor plan
(G) visualization
(H) storyboard

(I) production schedule
(J) AD
(K) DP

1. an especially vivid mental image—visual or aural—during script analysis that determines the subsequent visualizations and sequencing

2. a breakdown of time blocks for various activities on the actual production day

3. the calendar that shows the preproduction, production, and postproduction dates and who is doing what, when, and where

1 ○ A ○ B ○ C ○ D
   ○ E ○ F ○ G ○ H
   ○ I ○ J ○ K

2 ○ A ○ B ○ C ○ D
   ○ E ○ F ○ G ○ H
   ○ I ○ J ○ K

3 ○ A ○ B ○ C ○ D
   ○ E ○ F ○ G ○ H
   ○ I ○ J ○ K

PAGE TOTAL _____

(A) time line	(E) sequencing	(I) production schedule
(B) location sketch	(F) floor plan	(J) AD
(C) facilities request	(G) visualization	(K) DP
(D) locking-in	(H) storyboard	

4. a series of sketches of the key shots

4
○ ○ ○ ○
A B C D
○ ○ ○ ○
E F G H
○ ○ ○
I J K

5. the control and the structuring of a series of shots during editing

5
○ ○ ○ ○
A B C D
○ ○ ○ ○
E F G H
○ ○ ○
I J K

6. a list that contains all technical facilities needed for a specific production

6
○ ○ ○ ○
A B C D
○ ○ ○ ○
E F G H
○ ○ ○
I J K

7. the mental image of a shot or several key images of a sequence

7
○ ○ ○ ○
A B C D
○ ○ ○ ○
E F G H
○ ○ ○
I J K

8. a rough map of the locale of a remote shoot

8
○ ○ ○ ○
A B C D
○ ○ ○ ○
E F G H
○ ○ ○
I J K

P A G E
T O T A L

9. the person who assists the director

9 ◯ ◯ ◯ ◯
   A B C D
   ◯ ◯ ◯ ◯
   E F G H
   ◯ ◯ ◯
   I J K

10. a diagram that shows scenery and major props

10 ◯ ◯ ◯ ◯
   A B C D
   ◯ ◯ ◯ ◯
   E F G H
   ◯ ◯ ◯
   I J K

11. the person who does the lighting (in cinema) and also operates the camera (in EFP)

11 ◯ ◯ ◯ ◯
   A B C D
   ◯ ◯ ◯ ◯
   E F G H
   ◯ ◯ ◯
   I J K

PAGE
TOTAL [ ]

SECTION
TOTAL [ ]

REVIEW OF PROCESS MESSAGE AND PRODUCTION METHOD

1. Evaluate to what extent the following four defined process messages will (A) *help* (B) *not help* you visualize key show elements and provide (C) *clear* (D) *only very few or no* clues to the various medium requirements. ***(Fill in two bubbles.)***

a. The program should show five different ways a family can conserve water during their morning shower and grooming.

1a ○ A ○ B ○ C ○ D

b. The program should demonstrate to the target audience (daily commuters) the benefits of turn signals and the consequences of ignoring them in rush-hour traffic.

1b ○ A ○ B ○ C ○ D

c. This program is a series of comedy shows.

1c ○ A ○ B ○ C ○ D

d. The program should show racecar drivers.

1d ○ A ○ B ○ C ○ D

e. The program should make non–sports viewers admire, if not feel, the ballet-like skills of basketball players.

1e ○ A ○ B ○ C ○ D

f. The program should help people conserve water.

1f ○ A ○ B ○ C ○ D

g. The program should make people drive better.

1g ○ A ○ B ○ C ○ D

h. The program should help children learn about safety when walking to school.

1h ○ A ○ B ○ C ○ D

PAGE TOTAL

Select the correct answers and fill in the bubbles with the corresponding letters.

2. A defined process message should include (A) *a specific audience* (B) *specific production equipment* (C) *the intended effect on the audience.* (**Multiple answers are possible.**)

2 ◯ ◯ ◯
   A B C

3. The translation of process message into video images is greatly aided by (A) *location sketches* (B) *a storyboard* (C) *a floor plan.*

3 ◯ ◯ ◯
   A B C

4. Process message 1b suggests (A) *a series of location EFPs for extensive postproduction* (B) *a studio show* (C) *a single half-hour field pickup during which a videographer is riding with a highway patrol officer in rush-hour traffic.*

4 ◯ ◯ ◯
   A B C

5. Look at process message 1e. It suggests (A) *a recorded live pickup of a professional basketball game* (B) *an EFP with staged plays on a basketball court* (C) *a live game restaged in the studio.*

5 ◯ ◯ ◯
   A B C

PAGE TOTAL [ ]

SECTION TOTAL [ ]

REVIEW OF SCRIPT MARKING

1. Match each field-of-view designation with its appropriate full term by filling in the bubble with the corresponding letter.

(A)   cross-shot
(B)   over-the-shoulder shot
(C)   long shot

(D)   extreme close-up
(E)   medium shot
(F)   extreme long shot

(G)   close-up
(H)   medium close-up
(I)   two-shot

a. CU

b. MCU

c. MS

d. ELS

e. LS

f. X/S

g. 2-S

h. ECU

i. O/S

1a ○ ○ ○ ○ ○
    A B C D E
    ○ ○ ○ ○
    F G H I

1b ○ ○ ○ ○ ○
    A B C D E
    ○ ○ ○ ○
    F G H I

1c ○ ○ ○ ○ ○
    A B C D E
    ○ ○ ○ ○
    F G H I

1d ○ ○ ○ ○ ○
    A B C D E
    ○ ○ ○ ○
    F G H I

1e ○ ○ ○ ○ ○
    A B C D E
    ○ ○ ○ ○
    F G H I

1f ○ ○ ○ ○ ○
    A B C D E
    ○ ○ ○ ○
    F G H I

1g ○ ○ ○ ○ ○
    A B C D E
    ○ ○ ○ ○
    F G H I

1h ○ ○ ○ ○ ○
    A B C D E
    ○ ○ ○ ○
    F G H I

1i ○ ○ ○ ○ ○
    A B C D E
    ○ ○ ○ ○
    F G H I

PAGE
TOTAL

Select the correct answers and fill in the bubbles with the corresponding letters.

2. The shot sheet for (A) *camera 1* (B) *camera 2* is incorrect because it has (C) *consecutive shot numbers* (D) *discontinuous shot numbers* (E) *an unworkable shot sequence* (F) *insufficient information for the director.* (**Multiple answers are possible.**)

2 ○ ○
   A B
   ○ ○ ○ ○
   C D E F

C1

Shot #
1 CU of Kim
2 Follow her
3 Zoom To ECU
4 Truck left
5 Zoom in To CU of Kim
6 Dolly out

C2

Shot #
9   CU of Gary
12 O/S Gary/Kim
16 Follow Kim
20 MS door; pick up Kim leaving
21 Follow Frank coming in

PAGE TOTAL [   ]

3. Mark the following brief scene for a three-camera live-recorded studio production. Add any additional video cues you deem necessary. The scene takes place in the small office of a busy advertising executive. Draw a floor plan and prepare a shot sheet.

KIM
(Bursts into Gary's office)

Let's go for coffee.

GARY

I don't have time.

KIM

Oh, shucks, make time.

GARY

You seem to be in a good mood today.

KIM

I'm always in a good mood...

GARY

Especially when I'm around.

KIM

I'm not so sure about that...but, yes, let's go.

GARY

I really don't...

KIM
(Walks behind Gary's desk and starts kissing his neck.)

Don't what?

GARY

Forget it. Let's go.

(The telephone rings. Gary turns to answer it but then lets it ring. He puts his arm around her. They both leave the office.)

---

4. Mark the following show opening of a series on basic video production. Memorize the cues so that you can devote your attention primarily to the preview monitors rather than to the script.

```
VIDEO BASICS SERIES
SHOW NO. 7
RECORDING DATE: July 15
AIR DATE: August 15

VIDEO                        AUDIO

Opening Server 2             Music SOS (sound on source)
:08 sec

CU of Phil                   PHIL
                             Hi, I'm Phil Kipper. Welcome to the
                             Broadcast and Electronic Communication
                             Arts Series, "Video Basics." As
                             promised last week, we will take you to a
                             special room where magic takes place:
                             the editing suite.


Pull out to reveal           PHIL
editing suite. Phil          Let me introduce to you the magician in
introduces Hamid.            charge, Hamid Khani, whose official title
CU of Hamid.                 is senior postproduction editor.


2-shot                       (SAYS HELLO TO HAMID AND HAS
                             HAMID SAY HELLO TO THE AUDIENCE)
```

Select the correct answers and fill in the bubbles with the corresponding letters.

5. The script markings in the following figure are (A) *acceptable* (B) *unacceptable* because they (C) *are too small* (D) *have unnecessary or redundant cues* (E) *are in the wrong place* (F) *show large, essential cues.* **(Fill in two bubbles.)**

JOHN

What's the matter?

Ready camera 1
Ready to cue Tammy

TAMMY

Nothing.

Cue Tammy and
take camera 1

JOHN

What do you mean, "nothing"? I can feel something is wrong.

TAMMY

Ready to cue John
Ready to take camera 2

Well, I am glad you have some feeling left.

JOHN *Cue John and take*
camera 2

What's that supposed to mean?

TAMMY

Please, let's not start that again.

JOHN

Start what again?

TAMMY *Ready to take camera 3*
for a two-shot

Well, I guess it's time to talk. *Take camera 3*

JOHN

What do you think we have been doing all this time?

REVIEW OF INTERPRETING STORYBOARDS

1. Each of the following four storyboards shows one or several major problems. Fill in the bubbles whose letters correspond with one or more of these major problems: (A) *poor continuity and disturbance of the mental map* (B) *wrong field-of-view designation* (C) *wrong above- or below-eye-level camera position.* (*Note: Storyboards may exhibit more than one problem.*)

Storyboard a

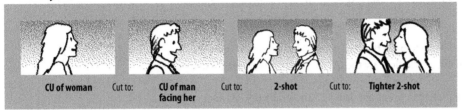

| CU of woman | Cut to: | CU of man facing her | Cut to: | 2-shot | Cut to: | Tighter 2-shot |

1a ○ A   ○ B   ○ C

Storyboard b

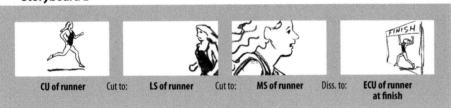

| CU of runner | Cut to: | LS of runner | Cut to: | MS of runner | Diss. to: | ECU of runner at finish |

1b ○ A   ○ B   ○ C

Storyboard c

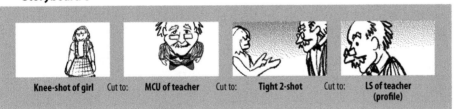

| Knee-shot of girl | Cut to: | MCU of teacher | Cut to: | Tight 2-shot | Cut to: | LS of teacher (profile) |

1c ○ A   ○ B   ○ C

Storyboard d

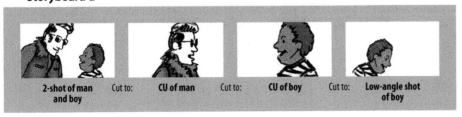

| 2-shot of man and boy | Cut to: | CU of man | Cut to: | CU of boy | Cut to: | Low-angle shot of boy |

1d ○ A   ○ B   ○ C

SECTION TOTAL [   ]

Identify the person mainly responsible for the following production activities and fill in the corresponding bubbles.

1. As the director, you want somebody to write down all major and minor problems that show up during rehearsal. For this job you would most likely ask the (A) *floor manager* (B) *producer* (C) *PA*.

   1 ◯ A ◯ B ◯ C

2. To put up and dress the new lawyer's set is the responsibility of the (A) *floor manager* (B) *art director* (C) *PA*.

   2 ◯ A ◯ B ◯ C

3. The novice news anchor would like to have the basic cues demonstrated. The cues should be demonstrated on the studio floor by the (A) *PA* (B) *floor manager* (C) *director*.

   3 ◯ A ◯ B ◯ C

4. In the absence of a property manager, props are usually handled by the (A) *floor manager* (B) *AD* (C) *art director*.

   4 ◯ A ◯ B ◯ C

5. In elaborate multicamera productions or digital cinema, some of the scenes are sometimes directed by the (A) *floor manager* (B) *AD* (C) *PA*.

   5 ◯ A ◯ B ◯ C

SECTION TOTAL [   ]

REVIEW OF TIME LINE

Select the correct answers and fill in the bubbles with the corresponding letters.

1. Each of these time line listings is (A) *acceptable* (B) *unacceptable* because (C) *the time allotted for this production activity is appropriate* (D) *it allots too much time for the specific production activity* (E) *it allots too little time for the specific production activity.* **(Fill in two bubbles.)**

   Time Line May 25: Live-recorded 20-minute interview with college president on a standard interview set. She brings a model of the new library building, which needs to be set up in an adjacent area.

a. 8:15 a.m.	Crew call	**1a** (A) (B) / (C) (D) (E)
b. 8:30–9:00 a.m.	Tech meeting	**1b** (A) (B) / (C) (D) (E)
c. 9:00–11:00 a.m.	Setup and lighting	**1c** (A) (B) / (C) (D) (E)
d. 11:00–11:30 a.m.	Lunch	**1d** (A) (B) / (C) (D) (E)
e. 11:30–11:45 a.m.	Notes and reset	**1e** (A) (B) / (C) (D) (E)
f. 11:45 a.m.–12:00 p.m.	Briefing of president (Green Room)	**1f** (A) (B) / (C) (D) (E)
g. 12:00–12:30 p.m.	Run-through and camera rehearsal	**1g** (A) (B) / (C) (D) (E)

   PAGE TOTAL [   ]

Each of these time line listings is (A) *acceptable* (B) *unacceptable* because (C) *the time allotted for this production activity is appropriate* (D) *it allots too much time for the specific production activity* (E) *it allots too little time for the specific production activity.* (*Fill in two bubbles.*)

h. 12:30–12:45 p.m.   Notes

1h A B
    C D E

i. 12:45–1:00 p.m.   Reset

1i A B
    C D E

j. 1:00–1:10 p.m.   Break

1j A B
    C D E

k. 1:10–1:45 p.m.   Record

1k A B
    C D E

l. 1:45–1:55 p.m.   Spill

1l A B
    C D E

m. 1:55–2:10 p.m.   Strike

1m A B
    C D E

Time Line June 2: Simultaneous multicamera shoot for postproduction of two songs by a local five-member rock group with a singer on a wireless hand mic.

n. 6:00 a.m.   Crew call

1n A B
    C D E

o. 6:15–6:35 a.m.   Tech meeting

1o A B
    C D E

P A G E
T O T A L

p. 6:35–7:00 a.m.   Setup and lighting

1p ◯ ◯
   A B
  ◯ ◯ ◯
   C D E

q. 7:00–9:30 a.m.   Production meeting

1q ◯ ◯
   A B
  ◯ ◯ ◯
   C D E

r. 9:30 a.m.–12:30 p.m.   First run-through with cameras

1r ◯ ◯
   A B
  ◯ ◯ ◯
   C D E

s. 12:30–2:30 p.m.   Lunch

1s ◯ ◯
   A B
  ◯ ◯ ◯
   C D E

t. 2:30–2:45 p.m.   Record first song

1t ◯ ◯
   A B
  ◯ ◯ ◯
   C D E

u. 2:45–3:30 p.m.   Notes and reset

1u ◯ ◯
   A B
  ◯ ◯ ◯
   C D E

v. 3:30–4:30 p.m.   Record second song

1v ◯ ◯
   A B
  ◯ ◯ ◯
   C D E

w. 4:30–5:00 p.m.   Spill

1w ◯ ◯
   A B
  ◯ ◯ ◯
   C D E

x. 5:00–6:00 p.m.   Strike

1x ◯ ◯
   A B
  ◯ ◯ ◯
   C D E

PAGE TOTAL ▢

SECTION TOTAL ▢

REVIEW QUIZ

*Mark the following statements as true or false by filling in the bubbles in the **T** (for true) or **F** (for false) column.*

		T	F
1.	In a properly scripted documentary, all audio information is on page-left and all video information is on page-right.	1 ○	○
2.	Experienced floor managers will cue on their own if they think the director has missed a cue.	2 ○	○
3.	Script marking is important when directing from a dramatic script and when directing from a two-column A/V script.	3 ○	○
4.	Proper visualization is essential for correct sequencing.	4 ○	○
5.	The drama script format requires the full dialogue of all actors but only a minimum of visualization cues.	5 ○	○
6.	A good floor plan will greatly facilitate camera and talent blocking.	6 ○	○
7.	Dramas are always fully scripted.	7 ○	○
8.	A storyboard shows the key visualization points of an event.	8 ○	○
9.	If the script marking simply indicates "(2)" for one shot and "(3)" for the next, it implies that no "Ready" cues need be given.	9 ○	○
10.	*Locking-in* means that you conjure up a vivid visual or aural image while analyzing the script.	10 ○	○
11.	Although the process message is important to the director in the production phase, it is relatively unimportant in preproduction.	11 ○	○
12.	A good storyboard helps the director visualize a shot and determine camera positions.	12 ○	○
13.	The time line is the responsibility of the PA.	13 ○	○
14.	Because the director is engaged in artistic activities, knowledge of technical production aspects is relatively unimportant.	14 ○	○
15.	When preparing camera shot sheets, the shots for each camera are listed in the order they appear in the script.	15 ○	○

SECTION TOTAL ☐

PROBLEM-SOLVING APPLICATIONS

1. The novice director proudly shows you, the producer, his marked show format for a live-recorded studio interview. He wrote out in longhand all the ready and take cues as well as all the cues for special effects. His writing takes up more space than the information of the show format. What is your reaction? Why?

2. The director of a number of successful digital movies tells you that "hearing" a shot can sometimes help the visualization process more than trying to "see" it. What does he mean by that?

3. The director of a live-recorded segment of a new situation comedy tells you, the producer, that she has great difficulty deciding on optimal camera positions and marking the script because the art director has not yet finished the floor plan. What is your reaction? What would you suggest?

4. While you, the director, are preparing an EFP of a documentary segment on the lumber industry, the producer tells you not to worry too much about shot continuity because he intends to put the show together in extensive postproduction editing. Do you agree with the producer? If so, why? If not, why not?

5. The director of a weekly live sports show (consisting of a host and a prominent guest) tells the producer that she does not need a detailed script but that a show format will do just fine. What is your reaction?

6. If you were to describe to the producer what *locking-in* means when reading a dramatic script, what would you tell him?

7. When asked to direct an on-location television adaptation of a hit stage play, you are advised that the play's theatrical director will determine the number and the positions of the cameras because he, after all, knows the stage blocking better than you do. What is your reaction? What would you suggest?

8. Mark two or three scenes of a dramatic script, first for a three-camera live-recorded studio production and then for a single-camera studio production. Note the differences.

9. Observe the scene while riding on a bus or train, waiting in line at an airport, eating lunch in a cafeteria, or sitting in a classroom while listening to a lecture. How would you re-create and intensify one or all of these scenes for a multicamera or single-camera production?

10. Prepare time lines for two studio productions and two EFPs.

5 The Television Camera

REVIEW OF KEY TERMS

Match each term with its appropriate definition by filling in the corresponding bubble.

(A) CCU
(B) camera chain
(C) resolution
(D) pixel
(E) raster

(F) white balance
(G) imaging device
(H) beam splitter
(I) field
(J) gain

(K) RGB
(L) frame rate
(M) analog
(N) digital
(O) sync generator

1. the scanning pattern of a video image

1	A	B	C	D	E
	F	G	H	I	J
	K	L	M	N	O

2. one-half of a complete scanning cycle

2	A	B	C	D	E
	F	G	H	I	J
	K	L	M	N	O

3. a prism within a camera that separates white light into the three primary colors

3	A	B	C	D	E
	F	G	H	I	J
	K	L	M	N	O

PAGE TOTAL

(A) CCU	(F) white balance	(K) RGB
(B) camera chain	(G) imaging device	(L) frame rate
(C) resolution	(H) beam splitter	(M) analog
(D) pixel	(I) field	(N) digital
(E) raster	(J) gain	(O) sync generator

4. equipment, separate from the camera head, that is used to achieve optimal video

4 A B C D E F G H I J K L M N O

5. a camera connected with the CCU, power supply, and sync generator

5 A B C D E F G H I J K L M N O

6. the sensor mechanism in a camera that changes light into electrical energy

6 A B C D E F G H I J K L M N O

7. the relative sharpness of the picture as measured by the number of pixels

7 A B C D E F G H I J K L M N O

8. adjusting color circuits in a camera so that it sees a white object as white under various lighting conditions

8 A B C D E F G H I J K L M N O

PAGE TOTAL

9. the smallest single image element

9 ○ ○ ○ ○ ○
   A B C D E
   ○ ○ ○ ○ ○
   F G H I J
   ○ ○ ○ ○ ○
   K L M N O

10. the basic colors of television

10 ○ ○ ○ ○ ○
    A B C D E
    ○ ○ ○ ○ ○
    F G H I J
    ○ ○ ○ ○ ○
    K L M N O

11. electronic amplification of the video signal, boosting primarily picture brightness

11 ○ ○ ○ ○ ○
    A B C D E
    ○ ○ ○ ○ ○
    F G H I J
    ○ ○ ○ ○ ○
    K L M N O

12. a signal that fluctuates like the original stimulus

12 ○ ○ ○ ○ ○
    A B C D E
    ○ ○ ○ ○ ○
    F G H I J
    ○ ○ ○ ○ ○
    K L M N O

13. the number of complete video frames the video system is producing each second

13 ○ ○ ○ ○ ○
    A B C D E
    ○ ○ ○ ○ ○
    F G H I J
    ○ ○ ○ ○ ○
    K L M N O

14. usually refers to the binary system—the representation of data in the form of binary digits

14 ○ ○ ○ ○ ○
    A B C D E
    ○ ○ ○ ○ ○
    F G H I J
    ○ ○ ○ ○ ○
    K L M N O

PAGE
TOTAL [   ]

(A) CCU	(F) white balance	(K) RGB
(B) camera chain	(G) imaging device	(L) frame rate
(C) resolution	(H) beam splitter	(M) analog
(D) pixel	(I) field	(N) digital
(E) raster	(J) gain	(O) sync generator

15. part of the camera chain; produces an electronic synchronization signal, which keeps all scanning in step

15   ○ ○ ○ ○ ○
     A B C D E

     ○ ○ ○ ○ ○
     F G H I J

     ○ ○ ○ ○ ○
     K L M N O

PAGE TOTAL

SECTION TOTAL

REVIEW OF BASIC CAMERA ELEMENTS AND FUNCTIONS

1. Fill in the bubbles whose letters correspond with the camera elements shown in the following figure.

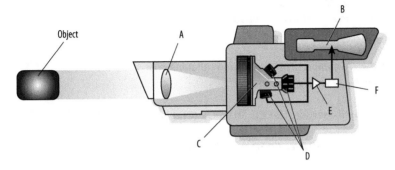

a. converts signals back into visible screen images

b. amplifies video signals

c. transforms light into electric energy or video signals

d. gathers and transmits light

e. splits white light into red, green, and blue light beams

f. processes video signal

PAGE
TOTAL [   ]

Select the correct answers and fill in the bubbles with the corresponding letters.

2. To adjust a studio camera to produce optimal pictures, the VO must operate the
(A) *CCU* (B) *CCD* (C) *HDV.*

2 ○ ○ ○
  A   B   C

3. Three basic parts of the camera chain are the (A) *power supply* (B) *prism block* (C) *lens*
(D) *sync generator* (E) *camera head* (F) *viewfinder.* **(Fill in three bubbles.)**

3 ○ ○ ○
  A   B   C
  ○ ○ ○
  D   E   F

4. An 8K digital cinema camera refers to the (A) *number of pixels per frame* (B) *number of
pixels on each horizontal scan line* (C) *number of vertical scan lines.*

4 ○ ○ ○
  A   B   C

5. One of the following names describes a specific sensor: (A) *CCU* (B) *CMOS* (C) *chip.*

5 ○ ○ ○
  A   B   C

6. The camera imaging device is also called the (A) *ND filter* (B) *SD card* (C) *sensor.*

6 ○ ○ ○
  A   B   C

7. In some cameras the prism block is replaced by a (A) *CCD* (B) *lens* (C) *striped or mosaic
filter array.*

7 ○ ○ ○
  A   B   C

PAGE
TOTAL

SECTION
TOTAL

REVIEW OF DIGITAL PROCESSES AND VIDEO QUALITY

Select the correct answers and fill in the bubbles with the corresponding letters.

1. Digital signals are based on the (A) *multiscan* (B) *binary* (C) *multipixel* system.

2. The scanning system of a sensor is a (A) *raster* (B) *scanning matrix* (C) *RGB grid*.

3. Which of the following diagrams most accurately represents a digital signal?

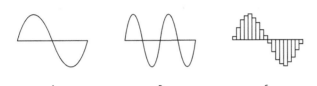

A   B   C

4. Digital television can use (A) *only progressive scanning* (B) *only interlaced scanning* (C) *both progressive and interlaced scanning*.

5. Spatial resolution is determined by (A) *the number of scan lines and pixels per line* (B) *frame rate* (C) *scanning speed*.

6. Temporal resolution is determined by (A) *the number of scan lines and pixels per line* (B) *frame rate* (C) *scanning speed*.

7. A high-fidelity digital signal requires a (A) *low sampling rate* (B) *high sampling rate* (C) *low pixel raster*.

8. In video, *shading* means (A) *creating shadows electronically* (B) *preventing the shadows from falling on certain objects* (C) *controlling contrast*.

9. The standard video system that delivers the sharpest pictures is (A) *720p* (B) *1080p* (C) *1080i*.

10. A high gain compensates for (A) *low light levels* (B) *low shutter speed* (C) *low voltage*.

11. A high electronic shutter speed will (A) *prevent a fast drain of the battery* (B) *put the camera in slow-motion mode* (C) *prevent blurring of fast-moving objects*.

12. To record in stereo 3D, the stereo 3D camcorder has (A) *one* (B) *two* (C) *three* identical cameras built into a single housing.

	A	B	C
1	○	○	○
2	○	○	○
3	○	○	○
4	○	○	○
5	○	○	○
6	○	○	○
7	○	○	○
8	○	○	○
9	○	○	○
10	○	○	○
11	○	○	○
12	○	○	○

SECTION TOTAL [＿＿＿＿]

*Mark the following statements as true or false by filling in the bubbles in the **T** (for true) or **F** (for false) column.*

		T	F
1.	An S-video cable does not carry audio signals.	1 ○	○
2.	An XLR plug is an audio connector.	2 ○	○
3.	Digital data can be transferred via Thunderbolt and HDMI cables.	3 ○	○
4.	Generally, studio cameras have higher-quality lenses than do ENG camcorders.	4 ○	○
5.	A CMOS chip is similar in function to a CCD.	5 ○	○
6.	The camera sensor transduces electrical energy into light.	6 ○	○
7.	RCA phono connectors can be used for digital video as well as audio signals.	7 ○	○
8.	A 720p scan always has a higher temporal resolution than a 1080i scan.	8 ○	○
9.	You can use an ND filter to reduce the intensity of bright light.	9 ○	○
10.	White-balancing adjusts the color circuits in the camera.	10 ○	○
11.	Digital signals are more robust but less complete than analog signals.	11 ○	○
12.	A complete scan from top to bottom of all raster lines produces a single field.	12 ○	○
13.	A high sampling rate preserves more of the original signal than a low sampling rate.	13 ○	○
14.	A digital signal fluctuates exactly like the original stimulus.	14 ○	○
15.	Studio cameras are powered through the camera cable.	15 ○	○
16.	Temporal resolution is increased with a higher refresh rate.	16 ○	○
17.	The focus-assist feature enlarges the center of the image to facilitate focusing.	17 ○	○
18.	Normally, a standard HDTV camera has a larger sensor than a DSLR camera.	18 ○	○
19.	Triaxial cables can carry a signal farther than a Thunderbolt cable can.	19 ○	○
20.	Interlaced scanning needs two scanning passes for a complete frame.	20 ○	○

SECTION TOTAL [   ]

PROBLEM-SOLVING APPLICATIONS

1. When on an ENG assignment, you are forced to shoot in an extremely dark environment. There is no time to turn on any auxiliary lights, and your camcorder is not equipped with a camera light. What, if anything, can you do to produce visible images however noisy they may be?

2. When moving from indoor studio lighting to midday outdoor light, the field reporter tells you not to worry about white-balancing the camera again because the outside light of the foggy day seems to match the studio lighting anyway. What is your response? Why?

3. When watching a rehearsal of a dance company, the TD expresses concern because the dancers wear white leotards while performing a number in front of a black background. Is the TD's concern justified? If so, why? If not, why not? What are your recommendations?

4. The TD tells the camera operator that a high shutter speed needs a considerable amount of light. What does the TD mean by *shutter speed?* When do you need a high shutter speed? How, if at all, is it related to light levels?

5. Draw and describe the parts of the camera chain and their primary functions.

6. The TD assures the director that he can use a USB 3.0 cable for connecting older equipment built for standard USB 2.0 cables. Is the TD's advice correct? If so, why? If not, why not?

7. Your client wants a stereo 3D recording of an approaching low-flying plane. You don't have a stereo 3D camcorder, but the TD tells you that you can simply mount two identical camcorders side-by-side to view and record the scene from slightly different angles. Do you agree with the TD? If so, why? If not, why not?

8. Your editor insists on all-digital equipment with as high a sampling ratio and as little compression as possible because your projects require extensive postproduction with a great number of complex effects. What is your reaction? Why?

9. The salesperson in a television store tells you that a digital television receiver can change the scanning standard regardless of how the signals were originally sent. Is she correct? If not, why not?

10. You have been asked to select one of the HDTV systems (720p or 1080i) for your television studio. Describe each and justify why you would choose one over the other.

6 Lenses

REVIEW OF KEY TERMS

Match each term with its appropriate definition by filling in the corresponding bubble.

(A) focal length
(B) fast lens
(C) slow lens
(D) normal lens
(E) depth of field

(F) f-stop
(G) aperture
(H) zoom lens
(I) calibrate
(J) field of view

(K) zoom range
(L) wide-angle lens
(M) digital zooming
(N) iris
(O) selective focus

1. to make a lens keep focus throughout the zoom

1 Ⓐ Ⓑ Ⓒ Ⓓ Ⓔ Ⓕ Ⓖ Ⓗ Ⓘ Ⓙ Ⓚ Ⓛ Ⓜ Ⓝ Ⓞ

2. lens opening measured in f-stops

2 Ⓐ Ⓑ Ⓒ Ⓓ Ⓔ Ⓕ Ⓖ Ⓗ Ⓘ Ⓙ Ⓚ Ⓛ Ⓜ Ⓝ Ⓞ

3. the area in which all objects, located at different distances from the camera, appear sharp and clear

3 Ⓐ Ⓑ Ⓒ Ⓓ Ⓔ Ⓕ Ⓖ Ⓗ Ⓘ Ⓙ Ⓚ Ⓛ Ⓜ Ⓝ Ⓞ

P A G E
T O T A L

(A) focal length	(F) f-stop	(K) zoom range
(B) fast lens	(G) aperture	(L) wide-angle lens
(C) slow lens	(H) zoom lens	(M) digital zooming
(D) normal lens	(I) calibrate	(N) iris
(E) depth of field	(J) field of view	(O) selective focus

4. the general lens focal length that approximates the spatial relationships of normal vision

5. variable-focal-length lens, which can change from a wide shot to a close-up and vice versa in one continuous movement

6. the extent of a scene that is visible through a particular lens

7. the distance from the optical center of the lens to the front surface of the camera imaging device

8. a lens that at its maximum aperture permits a relatively small amount of light to enter and pass through

PAGE TOTAL

9. same as short-focal-length lens, which gives a broad view of a scene

9 Ⓐ Ⓑ Ⓒ Ⓓ Ⓔ
  A B C D E
  Ⓕ Ⓖ Ⓗ Ⓘ Ⓙ
  F G H I J
  Ⓚ Ⓛ Ⓜ Ⓝ Ⓞ
  K L M N O

10. the calibration on the lens indicating the diaphragm opening—and therefore the amount of light passing through the lens

10 Ⓐ Ⓑ Ⓒ Ⓓ Ⓔ
   A B C D E
   Ⓕ Ⓖ Ⓗ Ⓘ Ⓙ
   F G H I J
   Ⓚ Ⓛ Ⓜ Ⓝ Ⓞ
   K L M N O

11. a lens that at its maximum aperture permits a relatively great amount of light to enter and pass through

11 Ⓐ Ⓑ Ⓒ Ⓓ Ⓔ
   A B C D E
   Ⓕ Ⓖ Ⓗ Ⓘ Ⓙ
   F G H I J
   Ⓚ Ⓛ Ⓜ Ⓝ Ⓞ
   K L M N O

12. shown in a focal-length ratio, such as 20:1

12 Ⓐ Ⓑ Ⓒ Ⓓ Ⓔ
   A B C D E
   Ⓕ Ⓖ Ⓗ Ⓘ Ⓙ
   F G H I J
   Ⓚ Ⓛ Ⓜ Ⓝ Ⓞ
   K L M N O

13. focusing on an object on the z-axis in a shallow depth of field

13 Ⓐ Ⓑ Ⓒ Ⓓ Ⓔ
   A B C D E
   Ⓕ Ⓖ Ⓗ Ⓘ Ⓙ
   F G H I J
   Ⓚ Ⓛ Ⓜ Ⓝ Ⓞ
   K L M N O

14. electronically enlarging the image to simulate a continuous change of focal length

14 Ⓐ Ⓑ Ⓒ Ⓓ Ⓔ
   A B C D E
   Ⓕ Ⓖ Ⓗ Ⓘ Ⓙ
   F G H I J
   Ⓚ Ⓛ Ⓜ Ⓝ Ⓞ
   K L M N O

PAGE
TOTAL [   ]

(A) focal length	(F) *f*-stop	(K) zoom range
(B) fast lens	(G) aperture	(L) wide-angle lens
(C) slow lens	(H) zoom lens	(M) digital zooming
(D) normal lens	(I) calibrate	(N) iris
(E) depth of field	(J) field of view	(O) selective focus

15. the part of the lens that produces apertures of different sizes

15 ○ ○ ○ ○ ○
   A B C D E

   ○ ○ ○ ○ ○
   F G H I J

   ○ ○ ○ ○ ○
   K L M N O

PAGE TOTAL

SECTION TOTAL

REVIEW OF OPTICAL CHARACTERISTICS OF LENSES

Select the correct answers and fill in the bubbles with the corresponding letters.

1. Select the three variables that influence depth of field: (A) *focal length of lens* (B) *zoom speed* (C) *focus* (D) *camera-to-object distance* (E) *lens aperture* (F) *focus mechanism.* **(Fill in three bubbles.)**

2. In an optical zoom, the focal length is adjusted by (A) *shifting certain lens elements* (B) *shifting the pixels* (C) *moving the camera closer to or farther from the object.*

3. A *15x* zoom lens means that you can increase the focal length (A) *1.5 times* (B) *15 times* (C) *150 times* in one continuous zoom.

4. Zoom lenses used for sports coverage need (A) *a lower zoom ratio than* (B) *a higher zoom ratio than* (C) *the same zoom ratio as* those used for studio work.

5. Large apertures (iris openings) contribute to a (A) *great* (B) *shallow* depth of field.

6. The focal length of zoom lenses that are built into small camcorders is generally (A) *not long enough when zoomed in* (B) *not short enough when zoomed out* (C) *fixed while zooming.*

7. Compared with a slow lens and assuming maximum aperture, a fast lens (A) *transmits an image faster* (B) *transmits an image more slowly* (C) *permits more light to enter* (D) *permits less light to enter.*

8. A wide-angle lens has a (A) *short* (B) *normal* (C) *long* focal length.

9. Telephoto prime lenses, or zoom lenses in a narrow-angle position, have a relatively (A) *great* (B) *narrow* (C) *shallow* depth of field.

10. Compared with a fast lens and assuming maximum aperture, a slow lens (A) *transmits an image faster* (B) *transmits an image more slowly* (C) *permits more light to enter* (D) *permits less light to enter.*

11. The area in which all objects, although located at different distances from the camera, are in focus is called (A) *depth of focus* (B) *field of view* (C) *depth of field.*

12. In a digital zoom, the focal length is adjusted by (A) *moving the camera closer to or farther away from the object* (B) *shifting certain lens elements* (C) *cropping the image while magnifying it.*

1	A	B	C
	D	E	F
2	A	B	C
3	A	B	C
4	A	B	C
5	A	B	
6	A	B	C
7	A B C D		
8	A	B	C
9	A	B	C
10	A B C D		
11	A	B	C
12	A	B	C

PAGE TOTAL

13. Given a fixed camera-to-object distance, short-focal-length lenses, or zoom lenses in the wide-angle position, have a relatively (A) *shallow* (B) *wide* (C) *great* depth of field.

14. When calibrating the zoom lens, you (A) *zoom out all the way to a long shot, focus on the target object, and zoom back in again* (B) *zoom in all the way, focus on the target object, and zoom back* (C) *zoom in to the midpoint, focus on the target object, and zoom back.*

15. In the diagram below, select the most appropriate *f*-stop number for each of the four apertures (**a** through **d**) and fill in the bubbles with the corresponding letter.

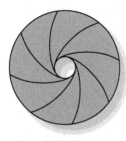

a. (A) *f*/ 5.6 (B) *f*/ 1.4 (C) *f*/22

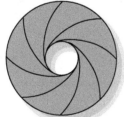

b. (A) *f*/16 (B) *f*/2.8 (C) *f*/1.4

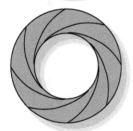

c. (A) *f*/1.4 (B) *f*/4 (C) *f*/16

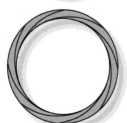

d. (A) *f*/ 22 (B) *f*/8 (C) *f*/1.4

REVIEW OF HOW LENSES SEE

Select the correct answers and fill in the bubbles with the corresponding letters.

1. To make a small room look larger, we use a (A) *wide-angle* (B) *narrow-angle* lens.

2. To apply selective focus, we need a (A) *great* (B) *shallow* depth of field.

3. Assuming that your image stabilizer is disengaged, you can avoid handheld camera wobbles by (A) *zooming all the way in* (B) *zooming all the way out* (C) *keeping the zoom lens in the narrow-angle position.*

4. A wide-angle lens (A) *increases* (B) *decreases* the illusion of depth and (C) *increases* (D) *decreases* the speed of an object moving toward or away from the camera. *(Fill in two bubbles.)*

5. The figure below shows the camera zoomed in all the way for a telephoto view and focused on object 1. Object 2 will probably be (A) *in focus* (B) *out of focus.* The depth of field is therefore (C) *great* (D) *shallow.* *(Fill in two bubbles.)*

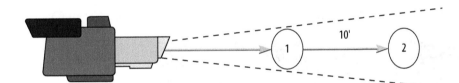

6. The figure below shows the camera zoomed out all the way for a wide-angle view and focused on object 1. Object 2 will probably be (A) *in focus* (B) *out of focus.* The depth of field is therefore (C) *great* (D) *shallow.* *(Fill in two bubbles.)*

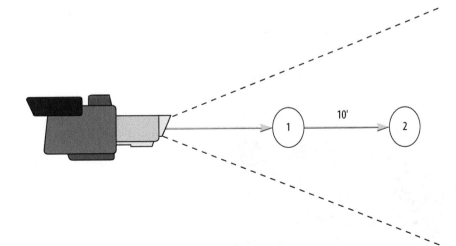

7. The closer the camera is to the object, the (A) *shallower* (B) *greater* (C) *wider* the depth of field becomes.

8. When zoomed in on somebody approaching the camera, the person seems to move (A) *slower than* (B) *about the same speed as* (C) *faster than* they actually do.

9. The screen image below displays a (A) *shallow* (B) *great* depth of field.

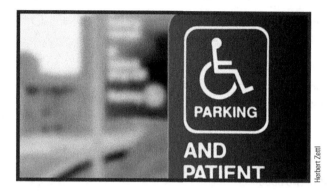

Herbert Zettl

10. The figure below simulates (A) *a digital zoom* (B) *an optical zoom*.

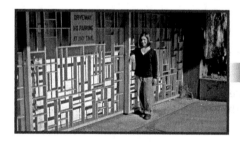 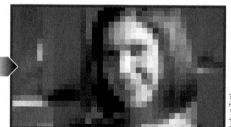

Herbert Zettl

11. In the screen image below, the zoom lens was in the (A) *normal* (B) *narrow-angle* (C) *wide-angle* position.

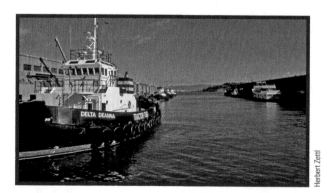

Herbert Zettl

PAGE TOTAL [   ]

76

© 2015 Cengage Learning

12. Your preview monitors for cameras 1, 2, and 3 display the following images. Assuming that all three cameras are positioned right next to one another, which is the approximate zoom position for each? Choose among (A) *wide angle* (B) *normal* and (C) *narrow angle*.

12 C1 ⭘ ⭘ ⭘
      A B C

C2 ⭘ ⭘ ⭘
    A B C

C3 ⭘ ⭘ ⭘
    A B C

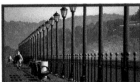

Camera 1

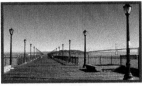
Camera 2

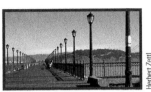
Camera 3

13. The screen image below shows that the camera's zoom lens was in a (A) *narrow-angle* (B) *wide-angle* position.

13 ⭘   ⭘
   A   B

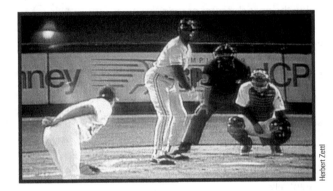

14. A narrow-angle lens makes objects positioned at different distances from the camera look (A) *more* (B) *less* crowded than they really are and (C) *increases* (D) *decreases* the speed of an object moving toward or away from the camera. *(Fill in two bubbles.)*

14 ⭘   ⭘
   A   B
   ⭘   ⭘
   C   D

15. The opening shot of a documentary on city politics shows the city hall through a piece of sculpture. The camera operator used (A) *a wide-angle* (B) *a narrow-angle* position.

15 ⭘   ⭘
   A   B

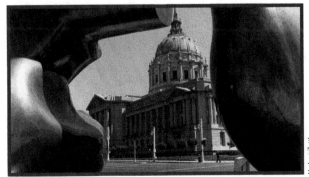

PAGE TOTAL [ ]

SECTION TOTAL [ ]

REVIEW QUIZ

*Mark the following statements as true or false by filling in the bubbles in the **T** (for true) or **F** (for false) column.*

		T	F
1.	Digital stabilizers can absorb all picture wobbles when you are shooting a narrow-angle picture.	1 ○	○
2.	When covering a news story with an ENG/EFP camera, you are best off with a shallow depth of field because there are few, if any, focusing problems.	2 ○	○
3.	Depth of field is influenced only by the focal length of the lens.	3 ○	○
4.	Depth of field increases as focal length decreases.	4 ○	○
5.	A zoom can be simulated by gradually enlarging the image's center portion.	5 ○	○
6.	A slow lens is one with a very low *f*-stop number, such as *f*/1.4.	6 ○	○
7.	An object moving toward the camera looks faster than normal when shot with a wide-angle lens.	7 ○	○
8.	When calibrating a zoom lens, you must first zoom in on the target object, focus, and then zoom out.	8 ○	○
9.	After the initial calibration of a zoom lens, you need to preset it again each time the distance from object to camera changes substantially.	9 ○	○
10.	Compared with an optical zoom, a digital zoom permits a higher zoom ratio without picture deterioration.	10 ○	○
11.	We can dolly most easily when the lens is in the maximum wide-angle position.	11 ○	○
12.	Each time you stop a zoom while zooming in, you get a different focal length.	12 ○	○
13.	Because a 1080i HDTV image has so many scan lines, the lens quality is relatively unimportant.	13 ○	○
14.	Digital and optical zooms work on the same principle.	14 ○	○
15.	Auto-focus and focus-assist are the same.	15 ○	○

SECTION TOTAL [   ]

PROBLEM-SOLVING APPLICATIONS

Let us now put the theory to work. You can observe the optical and performance characteristics of lenses easily by using a camcorder or a still camera that can accept various lenses. Think through each production problem and consider the various options, then pick the most effective solution and justify your choice.

1. Zoom all the way out with the camcorder, or attach a wide-angle lens (28mm or less focal length) to the digital single-lens reflex (DSLR) still camera, and focus on an object 4 to 6 feet away from you. Look at the background objects (20 or so feet away from you). Are they visible? Do they appear in fairly sharp focus? Or are they blurred? Now do the same observations by zooming all the way in or by attaching a telephoto lens (with a focal length of 200mm) to the still camera. Explain depth-of-field characteristics.

2. When watching television or a movie, try to figure out what lenses were used for some of the shots. For example, when you see someone running toward the camera yet seemingly not getting closer, what lens was used? Or when you see the happy couple approach the dinner table through the flowers and the candles in the foreground, what lens was probably used, assuming that the couple, as well as the candles and the flowers, are in focus? Such observations will help you become more aware of focal lengths and their effects.

3. You are the AD of a live telecast of a modern dance program, which is performed on a dimly lighted stage. The operators of the two key cameras express some concern about their lenses. The new lens of the handheld ENG/EFP camera 1 has a 25× zoom range and a maximum aperture of ƒ/5.6. Although the lens was used successfully during the past three football games, the operator feels that it might be too slow for this type of application. Camera 2 has a 10× lens with a 2× range extender. Its maximum aperture is also ƒ/5.6. Are the operators' concerns justified?

4. The novice director asks you, the operator of camera 3, to get the opening shot by zooming back slowly from an extreme close-up of the title of a book to an extreme wide shot that shows a large part of the studio (the other cameras, the floor manager, the overhead lighting) as the background for the opening titles. The director sets up the wide shot first to make sure that it shows enough of the studio. When the extreme-narrow-angle zoom lens position does not produce the desired close-up of the book title, he asks you to "simply pop in a range extender before we punch up your camera." What are the potential problems, if any? Be specific.

5. While shooting a dramatic program in the studio, the director tells you, the camera 1 operator, that your camera shows the scratched background walls in sharp focus. The director asks you to make the walls look slightly out of focus without impeding the sharp focus on the foreground talent. What would you do?

7 Camera Operation and Picture Composition

REVIEW OF KEY TERMS

Match each term with its appropriate definition by filling in the corresponding bubble.

(A) arc
(B) closure
(C) ELS
(D) headroom
(E) cant
(F) O/S
(G) POC

(H) studio pan-and-tilt head
(I) z-axis
(J) X/S
(K) leadroom
(L) dolly
(M) field of view
(N) interocular distance

(O) noseroom
(P) pan
(Q) rule of thirds
(R) tilt
(S) window
(T) truck

1. also called establishing shot

```
1   A  B  C  D  E
    F  G  H  I  J
    K  L  M  N  O
    P  Q  R  S  T
```

2. camera looks at the camera-far person with the back and shoulder of the camera-near person in the shot

```
2   A  B  C  D  E
    F  G  H  I  J
    K  L  M  N  O
    P  Q  R  S  T
```

PAGE TOTAL [   ]

(A) arc	(H) studio pan-and-tilt head	(O) noseroom
(B) closure	(I) z-axis	(P) pan
(C) ELS	(J) X/S	(Q) rule of thirds
(D) headroom	(K) leadroom	(R) tilt
(E) cant	(L) dolly	(S) window
(F) O/S	(M) field of view	(T) truck
(G) POC	(N) interocular distance	

3. similar to the over-the-shoulder shot except that the camera-near person is completely out of the shot

3
A B C D E
F G H I J
K L M N O
P Q R S T

4. to move the camera laterally by means of a mobile camera mount

4
A B C D E
F G H I J
K L M N O
P Q R S T

5. the space left in front of an object or a person moving toward the edge of the screen

5
A B C D E
F G H I J
K L M N O
P Q R S T

6. the point where the index vectors of the two lenses of a 3D camera intersect

6
A B C D E
F G H I J
K L M N O
P Q R S T

PAGE TOTAL

7. to tilt a handheld camera sideways

7 ○ ○ ○ ○ ○
   A B C D E
   ○ ○ ○ ○ ○
   F G H I J
   ○ ○ ○ ○ ○
   K L M N O
   ○ ○ ○ ○ ○
   P Q R S T

8. a variation of the golden section, wherein the screen is divided into three horizontal and three vertical fields

8 ○ ○ ○ ○ ○
   A B C D E
   ○ ○ ○ ○ ○
   F G H I J
   ○ ○ ○ ○ ○
   K L M N O
   ○ ○ ○ ○ ○
   P Q R S T

9. to point the camera up or down

9 ○ ○ ○ ○ ○
   A B C D E
   ○ ○ ○ ○ ○
   F G H I J
   ○ ○ ○ ○ ○
   K L M N O
   ○ ○ ○ ○ ○
   P Q R S T

10. the space left between the top of the head and the upper screen edge

10 ○ ○ ○ ○ ○
   A B C D E
   ○ ○ ○ ○ ○
   F G H I J
   ○ ○ ○ ○ ○
   K L M N O
   ○ ○ ○ ○ ○
   P Q R S T

11. imaginary line extending from the lens to the horizon

11 ○ ○ ○ ○ ○
   A B C D E
   ○ ○ ○ ○ ○
   F G H I J
   ○ ○ ○ ○ ○
   K L M N O
   ○ ○ ○ ○ ○
   P Q R S T

P A G E
T O T A L   [   ]

(A) arc	(H) studio pan-and-tilt head	(O) noseroom
(B) closure	(I) z-axis	(P) pan
(C) ELS	(J) X/S	(Q) rule of thirds
(D) headroom	(K) leadroom	(R) tilt
(E) cant	(L) dolly	(S) window
(F) O/S	(M) field of view	(T) truck
(G) POC	(N) interocular distance	

12. the name of the screen in 3D lingo

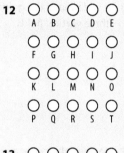

13. mentally filling in spaces of an incomplete picture

14. portion of a scene visible through a particular lens; its vista

15. the space left in front of a person looking toward the screen edge

PAGE TOTAL

16. mounting head for heavy cameras that permits extremely smooth movements

16
A ○ B ○ C ○ D ○ E ○
F ○ G ○ H ○ I ○ J ○
K ○ L ○ M ○ N ○ O ○
P ○ Q ○ R ○ S ○ T ○

17. horizontal turning of the camera

17
A ○ B ○ C ○ D ○ E ○
F ○ G ○ H ○ I ○ J ○
K ○ L ○ M ○ N ○ O ○
P ○ Q ○ R ○ S ○ T ○

18. to move the camera toward or away from an object

18
A ○ B ○ C ○ D ○ E ○
F ○ G ○ H ○ I ○ J ○
K ○ L ○ M ○ N ○ O ○
P ○ Q ○ R ○ S ○ T ○

19. to move the camera in a slightly curved dolly or truck

19
A ○ B ○ C ○ D ○ E ○
F ○ G ○ H ○ I ○ J ○
K ○ L ○ M ○ N ○ O ○
P ○ Q ○ R ○ S ○ T ○

20. the variable distance between two stereo lenses

20
A ○ B ○ C ○ D ○ E ○
F ○ G ○ H ○ I ○ J ○
K ○ L ○ M ○ N ○ O ○
P ○ Q ○ R ○ S ○ T ○

PAGE TOTAL [ ]

SECTION TOTAL [ ]

REVIEW OF CAMERA MOVEMENTS
AND CAMERA SUPPORTS

1. Fill in the bubbles whose letters correspond with the camera movements indicated in the following figure.

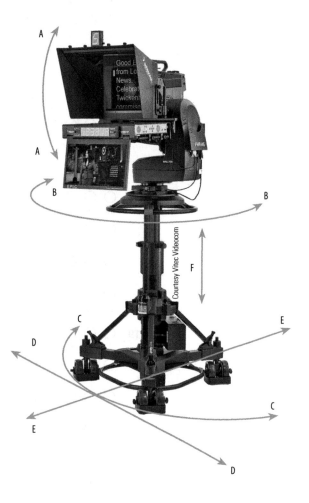

Courtesy Vitec Videocom

a. pedestal

b. truck

c. pan

d. tilt

e. dolly

f. arc

1a ○ A	○ B	○ C
○ D	○ E	○ F
1b ○ A	○ B	○ C
○ D	○ E	○ F
1c ○ A	○ B	○ C
○ D	○ E	○ F
1d ○ A	○ B	○ C
○ D	○ E	○ F
1e ○ A	○ B	○ C
○ D	○ E	○ F
1f ○ A	○ B	○ C
○ D	○ E	○ F

PAGE
TOTAL

Select the correct answers and fill in the bubbles with the corresponding letters.

2. Compared with a tripod, a studio pedestal allows these additional camera moves:
   (A) *canting left and right* (B) *raising and lowering the camera while on the air* (C) *booming up and down.*

   2 ○ A ○ B ○ C

3. Mounting heads facilitate (A) *dollies and trucks* (B) *smooth tilts and pans*
   (C) *arcs and zooms.*

   3 ○ A ○ B ○ C

4. A (A) *wedge mount* (B) *robotic pedestal* (C) *quick-release plate* makes it easy to detach
   an ENG/EFP camera from the tripod and reattach it again.

   4 ○ A ○ B ○ C

5. To simultaneously boom, tongue, pan, and tilt the camera, you need a (A) *robotic pedestal* (B) *jib arm* (C) *camera stabilizing system.*

   5 ○ A ○ B ○ C

6. The spreader (A) *keeps the tripod legs from spreading too far* (B) *must always be fully extended* (C) *helps spread the tripod legs as much as possible.*

   6 ○ A ○ B ○ C

7. The camera support that allows the operator of a small handheld camera to walk or run
   without any picture wobbles is a (A) *jib arm* (B) *monopod* (C) *handheld stabilizer.*

   7 ○ A ○ B ○ C

8. The camera support that allows the camera operator to run with the camera while
   keeping the picture steady is a (A) *robotic arm* (B) *Steadicam* (C) *jib arm.*

   8 ○ A ○ B ○ C

PAGE TOTAL [ ]

SECTION TOTAL [ ]

REVIEW OF HOW TO WORK A CAMERA

Select the correct answers and fill in the bubbles with the corresponding letters.

1. When panning with a shoulder-mounted ENG/EFP camera, you should point your knees toward (A) *the starting point of the pan* (B) *the end point of the pan* (C) *either direction.*

   1 ○ A ○ B ○ C

2. To minimize camera wobbles when dollying with a studio camera or walking with an EFP camera, the zoom lens should be in a (A) *narrow-angle* (B) *wide-angle* (C) *telephoto* position.

   2 ○ A ○ B ○ C

3. During a test recording with your ENG/EFP camcorder, you should (A) *leave the lens cap on but check the audio* (B) *make sure all camera features are working* (C) *ask the reporter to count to 10.*

   3 ○ A ○ B ○ C

4. When operating a camcorder in the field, you should always have the camera mic (A) *on* (B) *off* (C) *replaced by a shotgun mic.*

   4 ○ A ○ B ○ C

5. When dollying with a studio camera or walking with an EFP camera, the depth of field should be as (A) *shallow* (B) *great* (C) *narrow* as possible.

   5 ○ A ○ B ○ C

6. After having calibrated the zoom lens, you need to preset it again (A) *only when the camera moves* (B) *only when the object moves relative to the camera* (C) *whenever camera or object moves relative to the other.*

   6 ○ A ○ B ○ C

7. When calibrating a zoom lens, the tally light should be (A) *on* (B) *off* (C) *ignored.*

   7 ○ A ○ B ○ C

8. When on an ENG assignment, you should record ambient sound (A) *only if somebody is talking* (B) *only if there is no background noise* (C) *always.*

   8 ○ A ○ B ○ C

9. To achieve critical focus when operating an HDTV studio camera, you should (A) *adjust the viewfinder's sharpness* (B) *engage the auto-focus feature* (C) *engage the focus-assist feature.*

   9 ○ A ○ B ○ C

10. When loading a memory card for recording, the safety tab (A) *does not matter because it is primarily meant for playback protection* (B) *should be in the open position* (C) *should be in the closed position.*

    10 ○ A ○ B ○ C

11. You should lock the camera mounting head (A) *every time you leave it* (B) *only when temporarily leaving the camera* (C) *at the end of the shoot.*

    11 ○ A ○ B ○ C

12. When leaving a studio camera temporarily unattended, you should (A) *tighten the lock mechanism* (B) *tighten the drag control* (C) *point the camera toward the floor rather than into the lights.*

    12 ○ A ○ B ○ C

SECTION TOTAL [   ]

REVIEW OF PICTURE COMPOSITION

1. Evaluate the framing of the next five shots by filling in the bubbles with the corresponding letters. *(Note: There may be more than one correct answer for some parts of a problem.)*

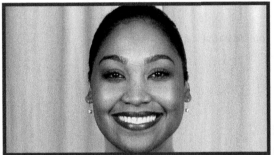

Edward Aiona

a. This shot is (A) *acceptable* (B) *unacceptable* because it has (C) *no headroom* (D) *too much headroom* (E) *no noseroom* (F) *no leadroom* (G) *insufficient clues for closure in off-screen space.* If unacceptable, you should (H) *tilt up* (I) *tilt down.*

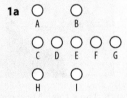

1a ○ ○
     A   B
     ○ ○ ○ ○ ○
     C D E F G
     ○ ○
     H   I

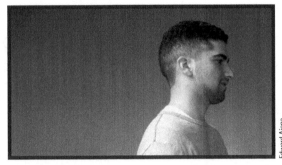

Edward Aiona

b. This shot is (A) *acceptable* (B) *unacceptable* because it has (C) *sufficient noseroom* (D) *insufficient noseroom* (E) *sufficient headroom* (F) *insufficient leadroom.* If unacceptable, you should (G) *pan left* (H) *pan right* (I) *tilt up* (J) *tilt down* (K) *pedestal up* (L) *pedestal down.*

1b ○ ○
     A   B
     ○ ○ ○ ○
     C D E F
     ○ ○ ○
     G H I
     ○ ○ ○
     J K L

P A G E
T O T A L [   ]

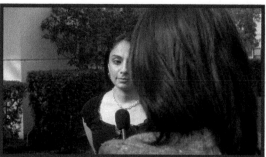

Edward Aiona

c. This over-the-shoulder shot is (A) *acceptable* (B) *unacceptable.* If unacceptable, you should (C) *zoom out* (D) *pedestal up* (E) *arc left* (F) *arc right.*

1c ○ A   ○ B
○ C ○ D ○ E ○ F

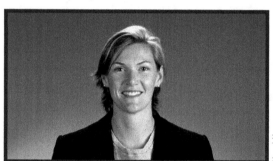

Edward Aiona

d. This CU is (A) *acceptable* (B) *unacceptable* because it has (C) *no headroom* (D) *too much headroom* (E) *adequate headroom* (F) *adequate noseroom.* If unacceptable, you should (G) *tilt up* (H) *tilt down* (I) *pan left.*

1d ○ A   ○ B
○ C ○ D ○ E ○ F
○ G ○ H ○ I

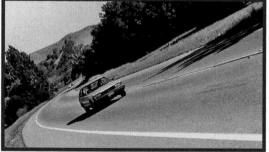

Herbert Zettl

e. This shot is intended to emphasize the car's speed and risky driving. Its framing is therefore (A) *acceptable* (B) *unacceptable.* If unacceptable, you should (C) *level the horizon line* (D) *zoom out.*

1e ○ A   ○ B
○ C   ○ D

PAGE
TOTAL

2. This shot makes (A) *good* (B) *poor* use of screen depth because (C) *it lacks foreground objects* (D) *the horizon is too high.*

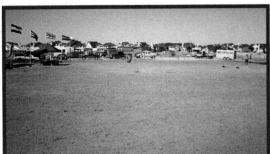

Herbert Zettl

2 ○ A   ○ B
       ○ C   ○ D

3. This framing is (A) *acceptable* (B) *unacceptable* in terms of closure.

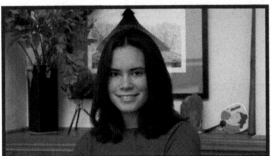

Edward Aiona

3 ○ A   ○ B

P A G E
T O T A L [   ]

4. Using the set of numbered images below, fill in the bubbles for each of the following fields of view or shot designations.

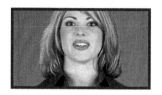

A

B

C

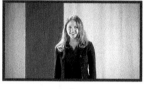

D

E

F

G

H

I

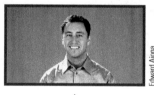

a. extreme close-up

b. knee shot

c. medium shot

4a ◯ ◯ ◯ ◯ ◯
    A B C D E
    ◯ ◯ ◯ ◯
    F G H I

4b ◯ ◯ ◯ ◯ ◯
    A B C D E
    ◯ ◯ ◯ ◯
    F G H I

4c ◯ ◯ ◯ ◯ ◯
    A B C D E
    ◯ ◯ ◯ ◯
    F G H I

PAGE TOTAL [ ]

Edward Aiona

d. over-the-shoulder shot

4d ◯ ◯ ◯ ◯ ◯
    A B C D E
    ◯ ◯ ◯ ◯
    F G H I

e. long shot

4e ◯ ◯ ◯ ◯ ◯
    A B C D E
    ◯ ◯ ◯ ◯
    F G H I

f. three-shot

4f ◯ ◯ ◯ ◯ ◯
    A B C D E
    ◯ ◯ ◯ ◯
    F G H I

g. extreme long shot

4g ◯ ◯ ◯ ◯ ◯
    A B C D E
    ◯ ◯ ◯ ◯
    F G H I

h. close-up

4h ◯ ◯ ◯ ◯ ◯
    A B C D E
    ◯ ◯ ◯ ◯
    F G H I

i. bust shot

4i ◯ ◯ ◯ ◯ ◯
    A B C D E
    ◯ ◯ ◯ ◯
    F G H I

PAGE TOTAL [ ]

SECTION TOTAL [ ]

REVIEW OF STEREO 3D

Select the correct answers and fill in the bubbles with the corresponding letters.

1. In stereo 3D, the z-axis (A) *goes only from the window to the horizon* (B) *extends both in front of and behind the window* (C) *goes only from the window to the viewer.*

2. The imaginary line representing an extension of the lens from the screen to the horizon is the (A) z_v-axis (B) z_h-axis (C) *3D axis.*

3. When the lenses are parallel and have no point of convergence, the entire event (A) *will lose its stereo effect* (B) *plays only along the z_h-axis* (C) *plays only along the z_v-axis.*

4. In stereo 3D, the rack-focus effect is (A) *an especially powerful means of emphasis* (B) *undesirable and confusing* (C) *effective so long as the lenses are synchronized.*

5. In stereo 3D, a cropped image floating in front of the screen is an example of (A) *closure* (B) *convergence* (C) *a window violation.*

6. In the figure below, select the POC that matches the 3D effect the viewer experiences.

1	○ A	○ B	○ C
2	○ A	○ B	○ C
3	○ A	○ B	○ C
4	○ A	○ B	○ C
5	○ A	○ B	○ C
6	○ A	○ B	○ C

A   B   C

PAGE TOTAL

7. In the figure below, select the interocular distance that matches the resulting stereo 3D experience.

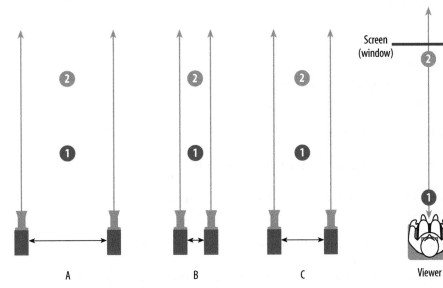

A   B   C   Viewer

Screen (window)

*Mark the following statements as true or false by filling in the bubbles in the **T** (for true) or **F** (for false) column.*

	T	F
1. To *boom up* means to raise the camera pedestal.	1 ○	○
2. Before the studio or remote production, you should check the tightest and widest field of view of the zoom lens from the principal camera position.	2 ○	○
3. Dolly and truck movements show up as similar movements on-screen.	3 ○	○
4. When both stereo lenses are fixed in a parallel position, all events play on the z_V-axis.	4 ○	○
5. Once balanced, the wedge mount ensures that the camera is mounted in an optimally balanced position for each subsequent use.	5 ○	○
6. The drag controls on a mounting head are used to lock down the camera.	6 ○	○
7. The interocular distance has no influence on the perceived length of the two stereo z-axes.	7 ○	○
8. When the entire event plays in the camera-far space of the point of convergence and the window is at the POC during projection, there is no z_V-axis.	8 ○	○
9. If your camcorder has an LCD foldout monitor, you should use it to focus whenever possible because it is bigger than the viewfinder display.	9 ○	○
10. Psychological closure always ensures good composition.	10 ○	○
11. The higher the zoom ratio, the more effective the lens is for studio work.	11 ○	○
12. A shallow depth of field is harder to handle in stereo 3D than in standard 2D photography.	12 ○	○
13. Leadroom and noseroom fulfill similar framing (compositional) functions.	13 ○	○
14. Field of view is expressed in abbreviations, such as *CU* for close-up.	14 ○	○
15. The studio pedestal permits very-low-angle shots.	15 ○	○
16. The jib arm and the camera crane can make the camera move in similar ways.	16 ○	○
17. The mark of experienced stereographers is heavy use of the z_V-axis.	17 ○	○

SECTION TOTAL [   ]

PROBLEM-SOLVING APPLICATIONS

1. Discuss the various cameras supports you use and point out their advantages and disadvantages. How can you overcome the disadvantages?

2. When using a fixed-lens camera (without interchangeable lenses), what is the most serious disadvantage? How does it influence your approach to production and camera handling?

3. The local high school asks you to recommend the cameras and the camera supports to rent for the live coverage of its championship football game. The coach reminds you that the budget is quite limited. How many and what type of cameras and supports would you recommend?

4. Pedestal up and down to see how high and low the camera will go. What can happen if you move the camera too fast to either end of vertical travel?

5. The director wants you to follow the new mayor up the flight of stairs in city hall without shaking the ENG/EFP camera. What camera mount would you suggest?

6. During the remote coverage of the World Computer Fair, the novice director tells you to zoom in to an ECU of a laptop display and then arc the tripod dolly around the display table to show the other computers. What are the potential problems, if any?

7. As you are leaving the studio, the producer states that a spare battery for your ENG/EFP camera is not needed because the story you are to cover will have, at best, a 20-second slot in the newscast. What is your response?

8. The producer tells you to be sure to keep enough headroom when framing an ECU. Do you agree? If so, why? If not, why not?

9. The director of his first 3D documentary asks you, the cameraperson, to be sure to keep the point of convergence between the two people in an over-the-shoulder shot. What is your reaction?

10. The same director insists on the widest possible interocular distance because he wants to use dramatic rack-focus effects. What is your reaction?

8 Audio: Sound Pickup

REVIEW OF KEY TERMS

Match each term with its appropriate definition by filling in the corresponding bubble.

(A) condenser microphone
(B) impedance
(C) omnidirectional
(D) ribbon microphone

(E) cardioid
(F) unidirectional
(G) phantom power
(H) polar pattern

(I) pickup pattern
(J) flat response
(K) frequency response
(L) dynamic microphone

1. a microphone whose sound pickup device consists of a thin band that vibrates with the sound pressures within a magnetic field

1 ○ ○ ○ ○
    A B C D
  ○ ○ ○ ○
    E F G H
  ○ ○ ○ ○
    I J K L

2. a microphone whose diaphragm consists of a plate that vibrates with the sound pressure against another fixed plate (the backplate)

2 ○ ○ ○ ○
    A B C D
  ○ ○ ○ ○
    E F G H
  ○ ○ ○ ○
    I J K L

3. a microphone that can pick up sounds better from one direction—the front—than from the sides or back

3 ○ ○ ○ ○
    A B C D
  ○ ○ ○ ○
    E F G H
  ○ ○ ○ ○
    I J K L

PAGE
TOTAL _____

(A) condenser microphone	(E) cardioid	(I) pickup pattern
(B) impedance	(F) unidirectional	(J) flat response
(C) omnidirectional	(G) phantom power	(K) frequency response
(D) ribbon microphone	(H) polar pattern	(L) dynamic microphone

4. the territory around the microphone within which the microphone can "hear" well, or has optimal sound pickup

4
○ ○ ○ ○
A B C D
○ ○ ○ ○
E F G H
○ ○ ○ ○
I J K L

5. a microphone whose sound pickup device consists of a diaphragm that is attached to a movable coil

5
○ ○ ○ ○
A B C D
○ ○ ○ ○
E F G H
○ ○ ○ ○
I J K L

6. a type of resistance to a signal flow: high-z or low-z

6
○ ○ ○ ○
A B C D
○ ○ ○ ○
E F G H
○ ○ ○ ○
I J K L

7. the range of frequencies a microphone can hear and reproduce

7
○ ○ ○ ○
A B C D
○ ○ ○ ○
E F G H
○ ○ ○ ○
I J K L

8. a specific pickup pattern of unidirectional microphones

8
○ ○ ○ ○
A B C D
○ ○ ○ ○
E F G H
○ ○ ○ ○
I J K L

PAGE TOTAL

9. the measure of a microphone's ability to hear equally well over its entire
frequency range

9 ○ ○ ○ ○
   A B C D
   ○ ○ ○ ○
   E F G H
   ○ ○ ○ ○
   I J K L

10. the two-dimensional representation of a microphone pickup pattern

10 ○ ○ ○ ○
   A B C D
   ○ ○ ○ ○
   E F G H
   ○ ○ ○ ○
   I J K L

11. preamplification power supplied by the audio console rather than a battery

11 ○ ○ ○ ○
   A B C D
   ○ ○ ○ ○
   E F G H
   ○ ○ ○ ○
   I J K L

12. a microphone that can pick up sounds equally well from all directions

12 ○ ○ ○ ○
   A B C D
   ○ ○ ○ ○
   E F G H
   ○ ○ ○ ○
   I J K L

P A G E
T O T A L [   ]

SECTION
T O T A L [   ]

1. Fill in the bubbles whose letters correspond with the polar patterns in the figure below.

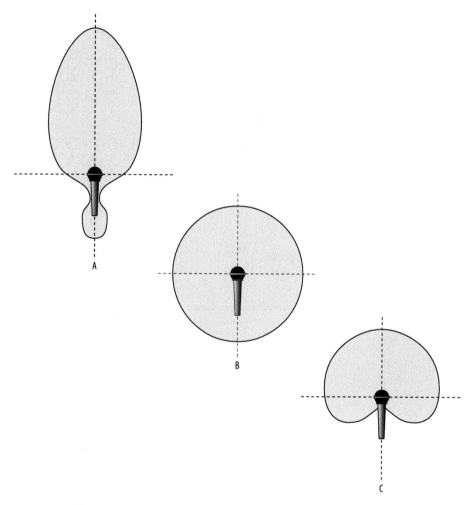

a. omnidirectional

b. cardioid

c. hypercardioid

	A	B	C
1a	○	○	○
1b	○	○	○
1c	○	○	○

P A G E
T O T A L

Select the correct answers and fill in the bubbles with the corresponding letters.

2. In general, dynamic microphones are (A) *equally sensitive as* (B) *less rugged than*
(C) *more rugged than* ribbon microphones.

2 ○ A   ○ B   ○ C

3. Normally, shotgun microphones have (A) *an omnidirectional* (B) *an extremely directional*
(C) *a nondirectional* pickup pattern.

3 ○ A   ○ B   ○ C

4. Select the three types of microphones as classified by their generating element:
(A) *dynamic* (B) *unidirectional* (C) *cardioid* (D) *ribbon* (E) *condenser* (F) *hypercardioid*.
(Fill in three bubbles.)

4 ○ A   ○ B   ○ C
   ○ D   ○ E   ○ F

5. The hand microphones used in ENG normally have (A) *an omnidirectional* (B) *a cardioid*
(C) *a hyper- or supercardioid* pickup pattern.

5 ○ A   ○ B   ○ C

6. Microphones that require a battery or phantom power for their output signal are
(A) *dynamic* (B) *ribbon* (C) *condenser*.

6 ○ A   ○ B   ○ C

7. The element in a microphone that converts sound waves into an electrical signal is the
(A) *sound-generating element* (B) *sound-amplifying chip* (C) *pickup device*.

7 ○ A   ○ B   ○ C

8. To eliminate sudden breath pops when speaking close to the microphone, we use a
(A) *pop filter* (B) *windscreen* (C) *frequency filter*.

8 ○ A   ○ B   ○ C

9. Faraway speech sounds are picked up best with (A) *a shotgun* (B) *an omnidirectional*
(C) *a ribbon* mic.

9 ○ A   ○ B   ○ C

10. The two-dimensional representation of a microphone's sound pickup area is the
(A) *safe area* (B) *polar pattern* (C) *pickup pattern*.

10 ○ A   ○ B   ○ C

P A G E
T O T A L   [   ]

S E C T I O N
T O T A L   [   ]

REVIEW OF HOW MICROPHONES ARE USED

Select the correct answers and fill in the bubbles with the corresponding letters.

1. The most appropriate mics for the voice pickup of a four-member news team (two anchors, a weathercaster, and a sportscaster) are (A) *lavaliers* (B) *desk mics* (C) *boom mics.*

   1 ○ A   ○ B   ○ C

2. For miking a kick drum, the microphone that is least subject to input overload has a (A) *ribbon* (B) *condenser* (C) *dynamic* sound-generating element.

   2 ○ A   ○ B   ○ C

3. The large shotgun microphone on a perambulator boom has (A) *an omnidirectional* (B) *a hyper- or supercardioid* (C) *a cardioid* pickup pattern.

   3 ○ A   ○ B   ○ C

4. The sound pickup of a brief scene of two people sitting at the dinner table is best done with a (A) *fishpole and pencil* (B) *fishpole and large shotgun* (C) *plant* mic.

   4 ○ A   ○ B   ○ C

5. When doing a live report from an accident scene, the most practical mic is a (A) *stand* (B) *lavalier* (C) *hand* mic.

   5 ○ A   ○ B   ○ C

6. When you are setting up the mics for a panel show, the audio engineer advises you to place them in such a way that they will not cause "multiple-microphone interference." This means that the mics must be placed so that they will not (A) *block the faces of the panel members* (B) *cancel some of one another's frequencies* (C) *multiply the ambient noise.*

   6 ○ A   ○ B   ○ C

7. To achieve a good and efficient voice pickup during the video-recording of four people sitting around a table in a small office, talking about effective sound handling in ENG/EFP, you should use a (A) *parabolic reflector* (B) *boundary* (C) *large shotgun* mic.

   7 ○ A   ○ B   ○ C

8. Parabolic microphones are especially effective for picking up (A) *especially soft* (B) *faraway* (C) *extremely close* sounds.

   8 ○ A   ○ B   ○ C

9. You are to set up microphones for a six-member panel discussion. All participants sit in a row at a table. Normally, you would use (A) *desk* (B) *hand* (C) *boom* mics for this production.

   9 ○ A   ○ B   ○ C

10. For the optimal pickup of an acoustic guitar, you should use a (A) *dynamic* (B) *condenser* (C) *dynamic cardioid* microphone.

   10 ○ A   ○ B   ○ C

SECTION TOTAL [   ]

REVIEW QUIZ

Mark the following statements as true or false by filling in the bubbles in the **T** *(for true) or* **F** *(for false) column.*

	T	F
1	○	○

1. Once a microphone is turned off, it is relatively immune to physical shock.

2. A hand mic clipped to a desk stand can serve as a desk mic.

3. The parabolic reflector microphone is especially appropriate for intimate, high-quality sound pickup with a high degree of sound presence.

4. Because lavalier microphones are highly sensitive, they work best when hidden under a shirt or blouse.

5. Condenser mics are especially good for the pickup of a bass drum.

6. A windsock fulfills the identical function as a pop filter.

7. Because wireless microphones operate on their own frequency, they are immune to interference from other radio frequencies.

8. If two desk microphones are too close together, their sound pickup may be compromised by multiple-microphone interference.

9. All professional microphones use three-pronged XLR connectors.

10. Blowing into a microphone is a good way to test whether it is turned on.

11. Dynamic mics are generally less sensitive to shock and temperature extremes than are ribbon mics.

12. Lavaliers can have a dynamic or condenser sound-generating element.

13. Because the boundary, or pressure zone, microphone needs a sound-reflecting surface, it should not be used as a hanging mic.

14. *Dual redundancy* refers to a backup microphone in case the first mic fails.

15. Feedback is the return to the musicians of the total or partial audio mix from the mixing console.

16. The pickup pattern of a system mic can be changed by attaching a different head.

	T	F
2	○	○
3	○	○
4	○	○
5	○	○
6	○	○
7	○	○
8	○	○
9	○	○
10	○	○
11	○	○
12	○	○
13	○	○
14	○	○
15	○	○
16	○	○

SECTION TOTAL _____

PROBLEM-SOLVING APPLICATIONS

1. You are responsible for the audio pickup of the live remote coverage at the airport during the Thanksgiving rush. Basically, you will have a reporter walking among the people waiting at the ticket counters, briefly interviewing some of the travelers. What type of mic would you use? Why?

2. You are in charge of audio for a show that consists of several intimate numbers by a singer and a small band. After the rehearsal an observer in the control room tells you that the singer holds the mic much too close to her mouth and that she should hold the mic lower and sing *across* rather than *into* it. What is your reaction? Why?

3. You are to provide optimal sound pickup for a preschool children's live-recorded show. The show consists of a host who moves among five to seven children seated on little chairs. The chairs are grouped around a small rug on which the children also play or dance from time to time. The dance music and other recorded audio portions are piped into the studio through the SA system. What microphone setup would you suggest for the host and the children? What problems might the SA system cause, if any?

4. An official at your former high school asks you to help with the audio for the championship basketball game. Somehow, so the official claims, the visiting spectators seem much louder on television than the home audience, although the latter is actually much larger and noisier than the guests. What can you do to accurately reflect the supportive cheering of the two sides? What specific microphone setups would you use?

5. You are doing a documentary on police patrols in your city. You first want to hear the conversation and the police radio inside the patrol car and then capture the sounds of conversations, yelling, or any other audio when the officers leave the patrol car to confront a suspect. What microphones would you need for optimal sound pickup in these situations?

6. You are to conduct an interview with the university president in her office. What microphones would you use? Why?

7. You are responsible for the pickup of an important live interview with a famous musician. The TD urges you to be sure to have an effective backup in case one of your lavalier mics fails. What is the easiest way to do this?

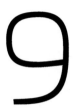 **Audio: Sound Control**

REVIEW OF KEY TERMS

Match each term with its appropriate definition by filling in the corresponding bubble.

(A) sound perspective   (E) mix   (I) VU meter
(B) patching   (F) equalization   (J) calibrate
(C) ambience   (G) AGC   (K) figure/ground
(D) sweetening   (H) PPM   (L) spatial sound

1. a means to connect various inputs with specific outputs

```
1   ○   ○   ○   ○
    A   B   C   D
    ○   ○   ○   ○
    E   F   G   H
    ○   ○   ○   ○
    I   J   K   L
```

2. emphasizing the most important sound source over other sounds

```
2   ○   ○   ○   ○
    A   B   C   D
    ○   ○   ○   ○
    E   F   G   H
    ○   ○   ○   ○
    I   J   K   L
```

3. a variety of quality adjustments of recorded sound in postproduction

```
3   ○   ○   ○   ○
    A   B   C   D
    ○   ○   ○   ○
    E   F   G   H
    ○   ○   ○   ○
    I   J   K   L
```

```
P A G E
T O T A L   [        ]
```

(A) sound perspective	(E) mix	(I) VU meter
(B) patching	(F) equalization	(J) calibrate
(C) ambience	(G) AGC	(K) figure/ground
(D) sweetening	(H) PPM	(L) spatial sound

4. regulates the audio or video levels automatically, without using pots

4
○ ○ ○ ○
A B C D
○ ○ ○ ○
E F G H
○ ○ ○ ○
I J K L

5. controlling the audio signal by emphasizing certain frequencies and eliminating others

5
○ ○ ○ ○
A B C D
○ ○ ○ ○
E F G H
○ ○ ○ ○
I J K L

6. to combine two or more sounds in specific proportions as determined by the event context

6
○ ○ ○ ○
A B C D
○ ○ ○ ○
E F G H
○ ○ ○ ○
I J K L

7. far sounds go with long shots; close sounds with close-ups

7
○ ○ ○ ○
A B C D
○ ○ ○ ○
E F G H
○ ○ ○ ○
I J K L

8. making all VU meters respond in the same way to a specific audio signal

8
○ ○ ○ ○
A B C D
○ ○ ○ ○
E F G H
○ ○ ○ ○
I J K L

PAGE TOTAL

9. helps define screen space

9 ○ ○ ○ ○
   A B C D
   ○ ○ ○ ○
   E F G H
   ○ ○ ○ ○
   I J K L

10. measures the relative loudness of amplified sound

10 ○ ○ ○ ○
    A B C D
    ○ ○ ○ ○
    E F G H
    ○ ○ ○ ○
    I J K L

11. meter in an audio console that measures loudness

11 ○ ○ ○ ○
    A B C D
    ○ ○ ○ ○
    E F G H
    ○ ○ ○ ○
    I J K L

12. environmental sounds

12 ○ ○ ○ ○
    A B C D
    ○ ○ ○ ○
    E F G H
    ○ ○ ○ ○
    I J K L

PAGE
TOTAL

SECTION
TOTAL

REVIEW OF STUDIO AND FIELD AUDIO PRODUCTION EQUIPMENT

Select the correct answers and fill in the bubbles with the corresponding letters.

1. A 16 × 2 audio console has (A) *16 inputs and 2 outputs* (B) *16 slide faders and 2 monitor systems* (C) *16 VU meters and 2 mix buses.*

2. The equalization controls on console modules (A) *bring all sounds to the same volume level* (B) *emphasize or de-emphasize certain frequencies* (C) *bring all incoming sounds to line-level strength.*

3. *Phantom power* means that the power is (A) *virtual but not real* (B) *not necessary* (C) *supplied by a source other than a battery.*

4. Most professional video- and sound-editing software lets you (A) *only see* (B) *only hear* (C) *both see and hear* the audio track.

5. A television audio console lets you (A) *synchronize audio and video in postproduction* (B) *punch up the audio source with the corresponding video* (C) *adjust the volume of each audio input.*

6. All professional video-editing systems let you control and mix (A) *only one audio track* (B) *two or more audio tracks* (C) *no audio tracks unless you interface it with special audio software.*

7. The trim control on the modules of studio consoles regulates the strength of the (A) *outgoing audio signal* (B) *final mix* (C) *incoming audio signal.*

8. When an incoming mic signal is routed to the line-level input, it (A) *will be distorted* (B) *must be amplified* (C) *may not need any volume adjustment.*

9. The appropriate place that marks the beginning of the "overload zone" is (A) *–5 VU* (B) *–2 VU* (C) *0 VU.*

	A	B	C
1	○	○	○
2	○	○	○
3	○	○	○
4	○	○	○
5	○	○	○
6	○	○	○
7	○	○	○
8	○	○	○
9	○	○	○

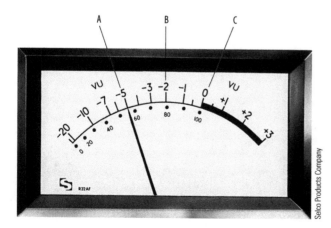

Selco Products Company

SECTION TOTAL [   ]

© 2015 Cengage Learning

REVIEW OF AUDIO CONTROL

Select the correct answers and fill in the bubbles with the corresponding letters.

1. The audio control tone, which gives a reference level of the recorded material, should be set at (A) *0 VU* (B) *+3 VU* (C) *–3 VU.*

    1 ○ A   ○ B   ○ C

2. The proper steps for audio system calibration are:

    2 ○ A   ○ B   ○ C

    (A)   1. *Activate the control tone on the console or mixer.*
          2. *Turn up the volume control for the incoming sound on the VR to 0 VU.*
          3. *Bring up the control tone fader on the console or mixer to 0 VU.*
          4. *Bring up the master fader on the console or mixer to 0 VU.*

    (B)   1. *Turn up the volume control for the incoming sound on the VR to 0 VU.*
          2. *Bring up the control tone fader on the console or mixer to 0 VU.*
          3. *Bring up the master fader on the console or mixer to 0 VU.*
          4. *Activate the control tone on the console or mixer.*

    (C)   1. *Activate the control tone on the console or mixer.*
          2. *Bring up the master fader on the console or mixer to 0 VU.*
          3. *Bring up the control tone fader on the console or mixer to 0 VU.*
          4. *Turn up the volume control for the incoming sound on the VR to 0 VU.*

3. The AGC (A) *discriminates automatically between figure and ground* (B) *works especially well in noisy surroundings* (C) *automatically boosts audio levels if they fall below preset levels.*

    3 ○ A   ○ B   ○ C

4. When recording sound during an outdoor EFP, you should (A) *filter out all ambient sounds* (B) *record ambient sounds on a separate track* (C) *plan to re-create the ambient sounds in postproduction.*

    4 ○ A   ○ B   ○ C

5. When using a CD player as an additional audio source, it must be connected to (A) *the mic input* (B) *the line input* (C) *neither the mic nor the line input* on the mixer.

    5 ○ A   ○ B   ○ C

6. Audio-system calibration normally refers to (A) *adjusting the audio input VU meter of the VR to the VU meter of the console output* (B) *adjusting the zoom lens so that it stays in focus* (C) *having the VU meter of the VR peak at a much higher level than the VU meter of the console output.*

    6 ○ A   ○ B   ○ C

    PAGE TOTAL [   ]

7. Recording several minutes of room tone or ambient sounds during a field production is especially important for (A) *establishing continuity in postproduction* (B) *helping set volume levels in postproduction* (C) *boosting aesthetic energy.*

7 ○ A   ○ B   ○ C

8. The least critical speaker placement in a 5.1 surround-sound system is the (A) *front-center speaker* (B) *front-side speakers* (C) *subwoofer.*

8 ○ A   ○ B   ○ C

9. Indicate the most common place to cut the digital audio track shown below.

9 ○ A   ○ B   ○ C

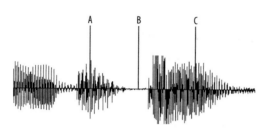

10. A memory card can store (A) *only analog* (B) *only digital* (C) *both analog and digital* audio signals.

10 ○ A   ○ B   ○ C

11. Taking a level is (A) *not necessary when the AGC is engaged* (B) *not necessary when recording digital sound* (C) *always necessary.*

11 ○ A   ○ B   ○ C

12. Which patches shown in the figure are correct? *(Multiple answers are possible.)*

12 ○ A   ○ B   ○ C
    ○ D   ○ E   ○ F

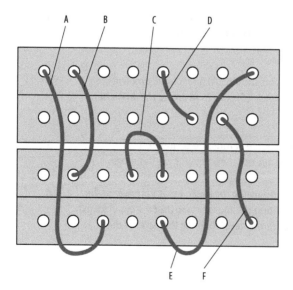

PAGE TOTAL [ ]

SECTION TOTAL [ ]

© 2015 Cengage Learning

REVIEW QUIZ

*Mark the following statements as true or false by filling in the bubbles in the **T** (for true) or
F (for false) column.*

		T	F
1.	In EFP we should try to mix all sound inputs as much as possible to minimize the need for postproduction mixing.	○	○
2.	The .1 speaker in the 5.1 surround sound system is the subwoofer.	○	○
3.	I/O consoles have an output channel for each input channel.	○	○
4.	The VU meter or the PPM will give an accurate reading of sound perspective.	○	○
5.	Environmental sounds are always interfering in EFP.	○	○
6.	Stereo sound defines the horizontal audio field.	○	○
7.	When recording digital audio, the master fader level should be kept somewhat below 0 VU.	○	○
8.	In contrast to large audio consoles, audio mixers have only one input but several outputs.	○	○
9.	An audio field mixer has quality controls similar to those of a console.	○	○
10.	On large multichannel consoles, each input channel has its own quality controls.	○	○
11.	Adding rhythmic sound is one of the primary techniques for establishing visual continuity.	○	○
12.	A solo switch on the console lets you listen to a single incoming sound while silencing all others.	○	○
13.	Small digital stereo recorders use memory cards for the storage of audio signals.	○	○
14.	*Sound perspective* refers to emphasizing the most important sound source over the general background sounds.	○	○

SECTION
TOTAL [   ]

PROBLEM-SOLVING APPLICATIONS

1. When setting up for video-recording a small rock group, you notice that the microphones and other audio sources exceed the number of inputs on the audio console. What can you do?

2. During rehearsal of the same production, you discover that the audio inputs that need the most attention are widely spread apart on the board. How can you get them closer together on the console so that their respective volume controls are adjacent to one another?

3. During a small segment of an EFP in an auto assembly plant, the novice director tells you to be especially careful to mix the ambient sounds and the voices of the reporter and the plant supervisor with the portable mixer so as to facilitate postproduction editing. What is your response?

4. During the digital recording of a concert, the VU meters occasionally peak into the +2 red zone. The director is very concerned about overmodulation. What is your response?

5. Some of the incoming audio signals during a rock concert are so hot (strong) that they bend the needle even at very low fader settings. What can you do to correct this problem without adjusting the source?

6. You have been asked to calibrate the audio system in your studio. Briefly describe the process step-by-step.

7. The director of the evening news would like you, the audio technician, to construct a playlist of all the bumpers for an automated and sequenced playback during the newscast. What piece of widely used audio equipment do you need to accomplish this assignment?

8. You, the audio technician, overhear the floor manager telling the anchorpersons that they do not need to be on the IFB system because it is, after all, his job to relay messages to the talent. What is your response?

9. How can you control the input levels before they reach the camcorder?

10. During postproduction the director insists on laying in a low but highly rhythmical music track, even under the dialogue, to boost the aesthetic energy of the scene. What is your reaction?

10 Lighting

REVIEW OF KEY TERMS

Match each term with its appropriate definition by filling in the corresponding bubble.

(A) gel

(B) incandescent

(C) softlight

(D) fc

(E) floodlight

(F) LED light

(G) reflected light

(H) barn doors

(I) fluorescent

(J) incident light

(K) dimmer

(L) spotlight

(M) baselight

(N) lux

(O) lumen

(P) Kelvin

(Q) white balance

(R) ND filter

1. a lighting instrument that produces diffused light with a relatively undefined beam edge

```
1   ○ ○ ○ ○ ○
    A  B  C  D  E
    ○ ○ ○ ○ ○
    F  G  H  I  J
    ○ ○ ○ ○ ○
    K  L  M  N  O
    ○ ○ ○
    P  Q  R
```

2. light that is bounced off the illuminated object

```
2   ○ ○ ○ ○ ○
    A  B  C  D  E
    ○ ○ ○ ○ ○
    F  G  H  I  J
    ○ ○ ○ ○ ○
    K  L  M  N  O
    ○ ○ ○
    P  Q  R
```

```
P A G E
T O T A L   [        ]
```

(A) gel	(G) reflected light	(M) baselight
(B) incandescent	(H) barn doors	(N) lux
(C) softlight	(I) fluorescent	(O) lumen
(D) fc	(J) incident light	(P) Kelvin
(E) floodlight	(K) dimmer	(Q) white balance
(F) LED light	(L) spotlight	(R) ND filter

3. a lighting instrument that produces directional, relatively undiffused light

3 ○ ○ ○ ○ ○
   A B C D E
   ○ ○ ○ ○ ○
   F G H I J
   ○ ○ ○ ○ ○
   K L M N O
   ○ ○ ○
   P Q R

4. even, nondirectional (diffused) light necessary for the camera to operate optimally

4 ○ ○ ○ ○ ○
   A B C D E
   ○ ○ ○ ○ ○
   F G H I J
   ○ ○ ○ ○ ○
   K L M N O
   ○ ○ ○
   P Q R

5. metal flaps in front of lighting instruments that control the spread of the light beam

5 ○ ○ ○ ○ ○
   A B C D E
   ○ ○ ○ ○ ○
   F G H I J
   ○ ○ ○ ○ ○
   K L M N O
   ○ ○ ○
   P Q R

6. an instrument that produces light through light-emitting diodes

6 ○ ○ ○ ○ ○
   A B C D E
   ○ ○ ○ ○ ○
   F G H I J
   ○ ○ ○ ○ ○
   K L M N O
   ○ ○ ○
   P Q R

PAGE
TOTAL [   ]

7. light that strikes the object directly from its source

7 ○ ○ ○ ○ ○
   A B C D E
   ○ ○ ○ ○ ○
   F G H I J
   ○ ○ ○ ○ ○
   K L M N O
   ○ ○ ○
   P Q R

8. American unit of measurement of illumination, or the amount of light that falls on an object

8 ○ ○ ○ ○ ○
   A B C D E
   ○ ○ ○ ○ ○
   F G H I J
   ○ ○ ○ ○ ○
   K L M N O
   ○ ○ ○
   P Q R

9. light produced by a glowing tungsten filament

9 ○ ○ ○ ○ ○
   A B C D E
   ○ ○ ○ ○ ○
   F G H I J
   ○ ○ ○ ○ ○
   K L M N O
   ○ ○ ○
   P Q R

10. the intensity of one candle (or any other light source radiating isotropically)

10 ○ ○ ○ ○ ○
   A B C D E
   ○ ○ ○ ○ ○
   F G H I J
   ○ ○ ○ ○ ○
   K L M N O
   ○ ○ ○
   P Q R

11. lamps that generate light by activating a gas-filled tube

11 ○ ○ ○ ○ ○
   A B C D E
   ○ ○ ○ ○ ○
   F G H I J
   ○ ○ ○ ○ ○
   K L M N O
   ○ ○ ○
   P Q R

P A G E
T O T A L [   ]

(A) gel	(G) reflected light	(M) baselight
(B) incandescent	(H) barn doors	(N) lux
(C) softlight	(I) fluorescent	(O) lumen
(D) fc	(J) incident light	(P) Kelvin
(E) floodlight	(K) dimmer	(Q) white balance
(F) LED light	(L) spotlight	(R) ND filter

12. European standard for measuring light intensity

12 A B C D E F G H I J K L M N O P Q R

13. floodlight that produces extremely diffused light

13 A B C D E F G H I J K L M N O P Q R

14. a device that controls light intensity

14 A B C D E F G H I J K L M N O P Q R

15. same as color filter

15 A B C D E F G H I J K L M N O P Q R

PAGE TOTAL [   ]

16. reduces incoming light without affecting color

16 ○ ○ ○ ○ ○
   A   B   C   D   E

○ ○ ○ ○ ○
F   G   H   I   J

○ ○ ○ ○ ○
K   L   M   N   O

○ ○ ○
P   Q   R

17. scale used to measure the relative reddishness and bluishness of white light

17 ○ ○ ○ ○ ○
   A   B   C   D   E

○ ○ ○ ○ ○
F   G   H   I   J

○ ○ ○ ○ ○
K   L   M   N   O

○ ○ ○
P   Q   R

18. camera adjustment to produce white in lighting of various color temperatures

18 ○ ○ ○ ○ ○
   A   B   C   D   E

○ ○ ○ ○ ○
F   G   H   I   J

○ ○ ○ ○ ○
K   L   M   N   O

○ ○ ○
P   Q   R

PAGE TOTAL [ ]

SECTION TOTAL [ ]

REVIEW OF STUDIO LIGHTING INSTRUMENTS AND CONTROLS

1. Fill in the bubbles whose letters correspond with the letters identifying the various parts of the spotlight shown below.

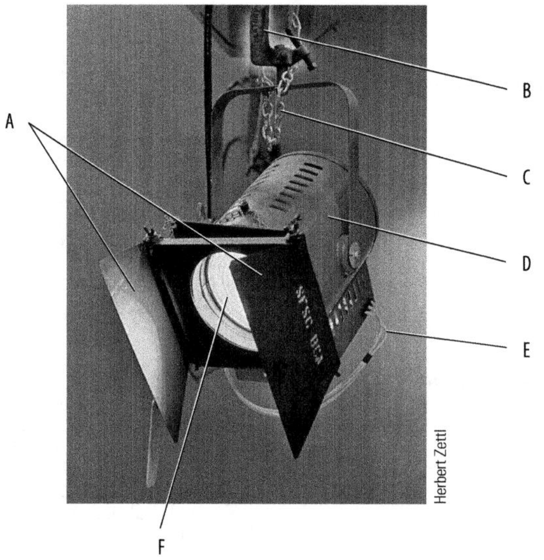

Herbert Zettl

a. Fresnel lens

b. two-way barn doors

c. C-clamp

d. power cord

e. lamp housing

f. safety chain

1a ○ A   ○ B   ○ C   ○ D   ○ E   ○ F

1b ○ A   ○ B   ○ C   ○ D   ○ E   ○ F

1c ○ A   ○ B   ○ C   ○ D   ○ E   ○ F

1d ○ A   ○ B   ○ C   ○ D   ○ E   ○ F

1e ○ A   ○ B   ○ C   ○ D   ○ E   ○ F

1f ○ A   ○ B   ○ C   ○ D   ○ E   ○ F

PAGE TOTAL

2. Fill in the bubbles whose letters correspond with the appropriate lighting instruments shown below.

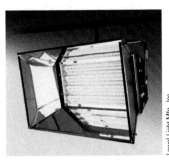

Lowel-Light Mfg., Inc.

A

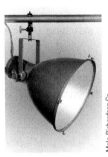

Mole-Richardson Co.

B

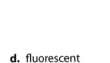

Mole-Richardson Co.

C

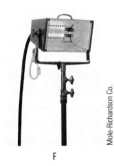

Herbert Zettl

D

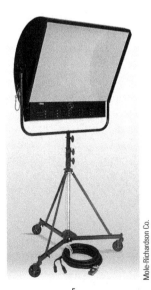

Mole-Richardson Co.

E

Mole-Richardson Co.

F

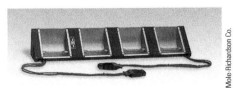

Mole-Richardson Co.

G

a. ellipsoidal spotlight

2a A B C D / E F G

b. softlight

2b A B C D / E F G

c. strip, or cyc, light

2c A B C D / E F G

d. fluorescent floodlight bank

2d A B C D / E F G

e. Fresnel spotlight

2e A B C D / E F G

f. scoop

2f A B C D / E F G

g. broad

2g A B C D / E F G

P A G E TOTAL

Select the correct answers and fill in the bubbles with the corresponding letters.

3. A dimmer controls the (A) *voltage flowing to the lamp* (B) *wattage of the lamp*
   (C) *amperes flowing to the lamp.*

   3 ○ A   ○ B   ○ C

4. You can make a fluorescent light beam somewhat directional by attaching (A) *an egg crate* (B) *a filter* (C) *barn doors.*

   4 ○ A   ○ B   ○ C

5. With the use of the patchboard (or computer patching), you (A) *must link only one instrument* (B) *can link several instruments* (C) *must link all available instruments simultaneously* to a specific dimmer.

   5 ○ A   ○ B   ○ C

6. To flood the light beam of a Fresnel spotlight, you need to move the lamp-reflector unit (A) *toward* (B) *away from* the lens.

   6 ○ A   ○ B

7. Scoops have (A) *a Fresnel lens* (B) *a plain lens* (C) *no lens.*

   7 ○ A   ○ B   ○ C

8. To diffuse the light beam of a scoop even more, you can attach (A) *an egg crate* (B) *a scrim* (C) *color media.*

   8 ○ A   ○ B   ○ C

PAGE TOTAL _____

SECTION TOTAL _____

REVIEW OF FIELD LIGHTING INSTRUMENTS AND CONTROLS

1. Fill in the bubbles whose letters correspond with the appropriate instruments shown below.

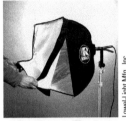

A

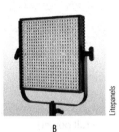

B

C

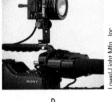

D

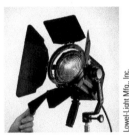

E

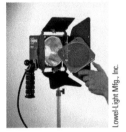

F

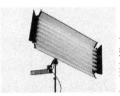

G

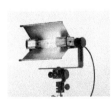

H

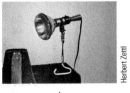

I

a. LED light

b. V-light

c. camera light

d. clip light

e. portable fluorescent bank

f. soft box

g. open-face spot

h. small Fresnel spot

i. Chinese lantern

1a ○ ○ ○ ○ ○
   A B C D E
   ○ ○ ○ ○
   F G H I

1b ○ ○ ○ ○ ○
   A B C D E
   ○ ○ ○ ○
   F G H I

1c ○ ○ ○ ○ ○
   A B C D E
   ○ ○ ○ ○
   F G H I

1d ○ ○ ○ ○ ○
   A B C D E
   ○ ○ ○ ○
   F G H I

1e ○ ○ ○ ○ ○
   A B C D E
   ○ ○ ○ ○
   F G H I

1f ○ ○ ○ ○ ○
   A B C D E
   ○ ○ ○ ○
   F G H I

1g ○ ○ ○ ○ ○
   A B C D E
   ○ ○ ○ ○
   F G H I

1h ○ ○ ○ ○ ○
   A B C D E
   ○ ○ ○ ○
   F G H I

1i ○ ○ ○ ○ ○
   A B C D E
   ○ ○ ○ ○
   F G H I

P A G E
T O T A L [   ]

Select the correct answers and fill in the bubbles with the corresponding letters.

2. The diffusion umbrella fulfills a similar function to (A) *a dimmer* (B) *a soft box* (C) *barn doors.*

3. The easiest way to reduce the light intensity of a portable spot is to (A) *use a small dimmer* (B) *use a smaller lamp* (C) *move the light farther away from the object.*

4. One common way to diffuse the light of an open-face spot is to (A) *attach a scrim to the barn doors* (B) *attach color media* (C) *use a dimmer.*

5. Portable light stands must always be secured with (A) *a safety cable* (B) *sandbags* (C) *counterweights.*

6. Excessive dimming of incandescent lights (more than 10 percent of full power) will (A) *not affect* (B) *decrease* (C) *increase* the color temperature. This means that the white light will (D) *remain basically unchanged* (E) *turn reddish* (F) *turn bluish.* **(Fill in two bubbles.)**

2	○ A	○ B	○ C
3	○ A	○ B	○ C
4	○ A	○ B	○ C
5	○ A	○ B	○ C
6	○ A	○ B	○ C
	○ D	○ E	○ F

PAGE TOTAL [   ]

SECTION TOTAL [   ]

REVIEW OF LIGHT INTENSITY, LAMPS, AND COLOR MEDIA

Select the correct answers and fill in the bubbles with the corresponding letters.

1. One foot-candle is approximately (A) *1* (B) *10* (C) *100* lux.

   1 ○ A   ○ B   ○ C

2. When measuring baselight, you need to read (A) *incident* (B) *reflected* (C) *directional* light.

   2 ○ A   ○ B   ○ C

3. When measuring incident light, you point the foot-candle or lux meter (A) *toward the set* (B) *toward the camera lens* (C) *close to the lighted object.*

   3 ○ A   ○ B   ○ C

4. When reading reflected light, you point the light meter (A) *into the lights* (B) *close to the lighted object* (C) *toward the camera lens.*

   4 ○ A   ○ B   ○ C

5. The beam of softlights (A) *can be adjusted by moving the lamp-reflector unit toward or away from the reflector* (B) *can be adjusted by attaching a Fresnel lens* (C) *cannot be sharply focused.*

   5 ○ A   ○ B   ○ C

6. To spot the light beam of a Fresnel spotlight, you need to move the lamp-reflector unit (A) *away from* (B) *toward* the lens.

   6 ○ A   ○ B

7. Colors can become distorted by (A) *inadequate baselight levels* (B) *low-contrast lighting* (C) *lack of shadows.*

   7 ○ A   ○ B   ○ C

8. Quartz lamps fall into the (A) *fluorescent* (B) *incandescent* (C) *HMI* category.

   8 ○ A   ○ B   ○ C

9. An advantage of LED lights is that they (A) *use less electricity* (B) *produce highly accurate color temperatures* (C) *are easy to dim.*

   9 ○ A   ○ B   ○ C

10. Most fluorescent tubes (A) *burn at exactly 3,200K and 5,600K* (B) *approximate the indoor and outdoor color temperature standards* (C) *burn with a neutral color temperature.*

    10 ○ A   ○ B   ○ C

SECTION TOTAL [ ]

REVIEW QUIZ

*Mark the following statements as true or false by filling in the bubbles in the **T** (for true) or **F** (for false) column.*

		T	F
1.	Incident light can be measured by pointing the light meter into the lights or toward the camera lens.	1 ○	○
2.	An HMI light needs an external ballast to function.	2 ○	○
3.	One effective method of turning a spotlight into a floodlight is to shine its beam into a diffusion umbrella.	3 ○	○
4.	A reflector can substitute for a fill light.	4 ○	○
5.	Portable fluorescent banks are used to illuminate areas with even light.	5 ○	○
6.	You can use egg crates to further spread the beam of softlights.	6 ○	○
7.	A flag has a similar function to barn doors.	7 ○	○
8.	Barn doors are primarily used for intensity control.	8 ○	○
9.	A sliding rod and a pantograph fulfill similar functions.	9 ○	○
10.	LED lights can be used to illuminate small areas for close-ups.	10 ○	○
11.	Focusing a light results in sharper shadows.	11 ○	○
12.	When necessary, the beam of softlights can be focused.	12 ○	○
13.	LED lights can change their light color without the use of color media.	13 ○	○
14.	The shutters on an ellipsoidal spot can shape its beam.	14 ○	○
15.	LED lights produce dense shadows.	15 ○	○
16.	The inverse square law is independent of how much the light is collimated.	16 ○	○
17.	To illuminate a large area with even light, you should use a variety of Fresnel spots.	17 ○	○

SECTION TOTAL [ ]

PROBLEM-SOLVING APPLICATIONS

1. You are asked to raise the baselight level in a classroom for optimal camera performance. Even though the small portable spotlights are in the maximum flood position, the additional illumination is not even. What other methods do you have available to achieve further diffusion?

2. You are asked to produce extremely sharp beams that reflect as precise pools of light on the studio floor. What type of lighting instruments would you use?

3. When checking the general baselight level and the amount of foot-candles (or lux) falling on the subject, the lighting assistant first stands next to the lighted subject and points the light meter toward the principal camera position. Will the assistant's action produce the desired results? If so, why? If not, why not?

4. You are asked to assemble a lighting kit that will be useful for lighting indoor interviews in small rooms, such as hotel rooms and offices. What instruments and other necessary equipment would you recommend?

5. You are asked to dim all spotlights simultaneously and then do the same thing immediately thereafter with all floodlights. How can you best accomplish this task?

6. The basketball coach of the local high school asks the television production teacher to flood the gym with HMI lights. What are your concerns, if any?

7. When video-recording a commercial for a local jewelry store, you are asked by the owner to try LED lights for illuminating a diamond ring because he wants a minimum of shadows. What is your reaction?

11 Techniques of Television Lighting

REVIEW OF KEY TERMS

Match each term with its appropriate definition by filling in the corresponding bubble.

(A) photographic lighting principle
(B) side light
(C) key light
(D) light plot

(E) fill light
(F) cameo lighting
(G) contrast ratio
(H) falloff
(I) background light

(J) kicker light
(K) low-key
(L) silhouette lighting
(M) high-key
(N) back light

1. the triangular arrangement of the three major light sources used to illuminate a subject

1 A B C D E   F G H I J   K L M N

2. the speed with which a light picture portion turns into shadow area

2 A B C D E   F G H I J   K L M N

3. unlighted subject in front of a brightly illuminated background

3 A B C D E   F G H I J   K L M N

PAGE TOTAL

(A) photographic lighting principle	(E) fill light	(J) kicker light
(B) side light	(F) cameo lighting	(K) low-key
(C) key light	(G) contrast ratio	(L) silhouette lighting
(D) light plot	(H) falloff	(M) high-key
	(I) background light	(N) back light

4. dark background, with a few selective light sources on the scene

4 ○ ○ ○ ○ ○
   A B C D E
   ○ ○ ○ ○ ○
   F G H I J
   ○ ○ ○ ○
   K L M N

5. illumination from behind and above the subject and opposite the camera

5 ○ ○ ○ ○ ○
   A B C D E
   ○ ○ ○ ○ ○
   F G H I J
   ○ ○ ○ ○
   K L M N

6. the difference between the brightest and the darkest portions in a picture

6 ○ ○ ○ ○ ○
   A B C D E
   ○ ○ ○ ○ ○
   F G H I J
   ○ ○ ○ ○
   K L M N

7. illuminates the set, set pieces, and backdrops

7 ○ ○ ○ ○ ○
   A B C D E
   ○ ○ ○ ○ ○
   F G H I J
   ○ ○ ○ ○
   K L M N

8. a diagram of scenery and major properties drawn on a grid

8 ○ ○ ○ ○ ○
   A B C D E
   ○ ○ ○ ○ ○
   F G H I J
   ○ ○ ○ ○
   K L M N

PAGE TOTAL [   ]

9. additional light that illuminates shadow areas and thereby reduces falloff

9 Ⓐ Ⓑ Ⓒ Ⓓ Ⓔ
A B C D E
Ⓕ Ⓖ Ⓗ Ⓘ Ⓙ
F G H I J
Ⓚ Ⓛ Ⓜ Ⓝ
K L M N

10. directional light coming from the side and the back of the subject, usually from below

10 Ⓐ Ⓑ Ⓒ Ⓓ Ⓔ
A B C D E
Ⓕ Ⓖ Ⓗ Ⓘ Ⓙ
F G H I J
Ⓚ Ⓛ Ⓜ Ⓝ
K L M N

11. light background and ample light on the scene

11 Ⓐ Ⓑ Ⓒ Ⓓ Ⓔ
A B C D E
Ⓕ Ⓖ Ⓗ Ⓘ Ⓙ
F G H I J
Ⓚ Ⓛ Ⓜ Ⓝ
K L M N

12. directional light from the side of an object

12 Ⓐ Ⓑ Ⓒ Ⓓ Ⓔ
A B C D E
Ⓕ Ⓖ Ⓗ Ⓘ Ⓙ
F G H I J
Ⓚ Ⓛ Ⓜ Ⓝ
K L M N

13. principal source of illumination

13 Ⓐ Ⓑ Ⓒ Ⓓ Ⓔ
A B C D E
Ⓕ Ⓖ Ⓗ Ⓘ Ⓙ
F G H I J
Ⓚ Ⓛ Ⓜ Ⓝ
K L M N

14. lighted subject in front of a dark background

14 Ⓐ Ⓑ Ⓒ Ⓓ Ⓔ
A B C D E
Ⓕ Ⓖ Ⓗ Ⓘ Ⓙ
F G H I J
Ⓚ Ⓛ Ⓜ Ⓝ
K L M N

PAGE
TOTAL [ ]

SECTION
TOTAL [ ]

REVIEW OF LIGHTING TECHNIQUES

Select the correct answers and fill in the bubbles with the corresponding letters.

1. The arrangement of the lighting instruments shown in the following diagram is generally called (A) *photographic lighting principle* (B) *four-point lighting* (C) *field lighting principle*.

2. Fill in the bubbles whose letters correspond with the functions of the lighting instruments shown in the diagram below and whether they are usually (S) *spotlights* or (F) *floodlights*.

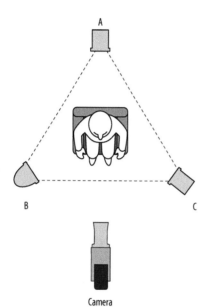

Camera

a. fill

b. back

c. key

1　○ ○ ○
　　A　B　C

2a　○ ○ ○
　　A　B　C
　　○ ○
　　S　F

2b　○ ○ ○
　　A　B　C
　　○ ○
　　S　F

2c　○ ○ ○
　　A　B　C
　　○ ○
　　S　F

PAGE
TOTAL

3. What major light sources were used to illuminate the host of a sports show in the following four pictures? In the diagrams, circle the instrument(s) used; then fill in the bubbles whose letters correspond with the instruments used to light the subject.

a.

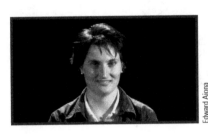

Edward Aiona

A

B

C

D

Camera

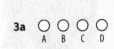

3a ○ ○ ○ ○
A B C D

b.

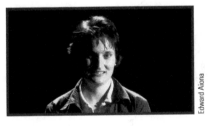

Edward Aiona

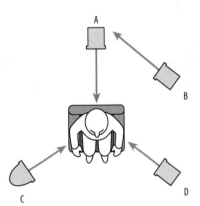

A

B

C

D

Camera

3b ○ ○ ○ ○
A B C D

P A G E
T O T A L

c.

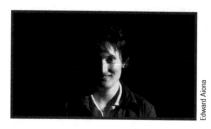

Edward Aiona

Camera

d.

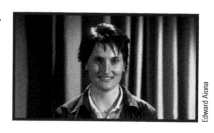

Edward Aiona

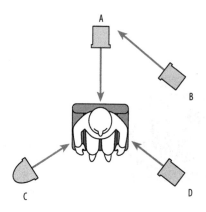

Camera

PAGE
TOTAL

4. You are to evaluate normal lighting setups. In the following six diagrams, cross out the lighting instruments that are unnecessary or most likely to interfere with the intended lighting effects; then fill in the bubbles whose letters correspond with the instruments *needed*.

a. chroma-key-area lighting

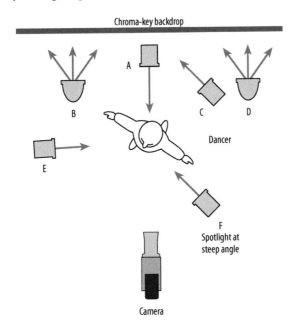

b. newscast

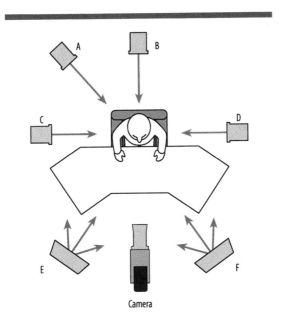

c. cameo lighting

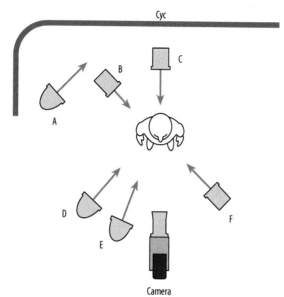

d. dancer in silhouette

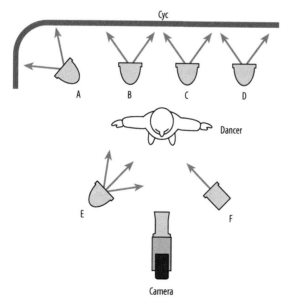

e. speaker and audience

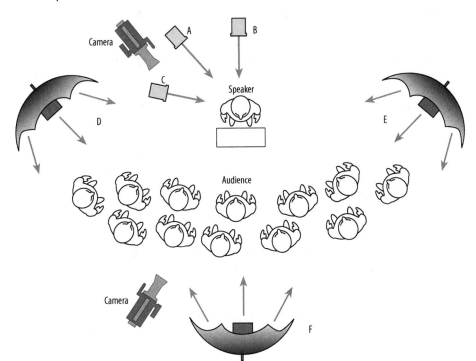

f. small still-life lighting

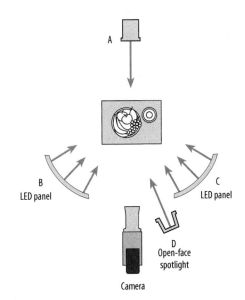

PAGE
TOTAL

© 2015 Cengage Learning

Select the correct answers and fill in the bubbles with the corresponding letters.

5. To make a model's hair look especially glamorous, you need a high-intensity (A) *key light* (B) *back light* (C) *background light.*

| 5 | ○ A | ○ B | ○ C |

6. To achieve a sharp shadow of a person cast onto a staircase wall, you need a (A) *focused Fresnel spot* (B) *Chinese lantern* (C) *softlight.*

| 6 | ○ A | ○ B | ○ C |

7. The standard color temperature for outdoor light in video is (A) *5,600K* (B) *3,600K* (C) *3,200K.*

| 7 | ○ A | ○ B | ○ C |

8. To achieve fast falloff, you need to use primarily (A) *spotlights* (B) *floodlights* (C) *fluorescent lights.*

| 8 | ○ A | ○ B | ○ C |

9. When shooting an ENG interview in bright sunlight, the most convenient fill light is (A) *an HMI spot* (B) *a quartz scoop* (C) *a reflector.*

| 9 | ○ A | ○ B | ○ C |

10. Having somebody stand in front of a brightly illuminated building will (A) *provide much needed back light* (B) *cause an undesirable silhouette effect* (C) *help separate the person from the background.*

| 10 | ○ A | ○ B | ○ C |

11. To light the backdrop for a chroma key, you need (A) *Fresnel spotlights* (B) *ellipsoidal spotlights* (C) *floodlights.*

| 11 | ○ A | ○ B | ○ C |

12. These lights fulfill similar functions: (A) *key and fill* (B) *back light and kicker* (C) *background light and kicker.*

| 12 | ○ A | ○ B | ○ C |

13. The usual power rating per circuit of ordinary household wall outlets is (A) *15 amps* (B) *50 amps* (C) *150 amps.*

| 13 | ○ A | ○ B | ○ C |

14. The color temperature of a light can be raised by using (A) *an orange gel* (B) *a light-blue gel* (C) *an ND filter.*

| 14 | ○ A | ○ B | ○ C |

15. To figure the total wattage that a circuit can safely carry, you should multiply the number of amps by (A) *15* (B) *75* (C) *100.*

| 15 | ○ A | ○ B | ○ C |

PAGE TOTAL [ ]

SECTION TOTAL [ ]

REVIEW QUIZ

*Mark the following statements as true or false by filling in the bubbles in the **T** (for true) or **F** (for false) column.*

		T	F
1.	Two side lights can function similarly to a key and a fill.	1 ○	○
2.	In most cases, a reflector can substitute for a fill light.	2 ○	○
3.	Plugging portable lights into different wall outlets means that they are automatically on different power circuits.	3 ○	○
4.	Triangle lighting uses a key light, a kicker light, and a back light.	4 ○	○
5.	The less fill light, the slower the falloff.	5 ○	○
6.	An LED panel simulates more a spotlight than a floodlight.	6 ○	○
7.	*High-key lighting* means that the key light strikes the subject from above eye level.	7 ○	○
8.	All cameo lighting is highly directional.	8 ○	○
9.	Low-key lighting is best achieved with low-hanging softlights.	9 ○	○
10.	*Low-key lighting* means that the lighting is soft and even, with extremely slow falloff.	10 ○	○
11.	Cast shadows can suggest a specific locale.	11 ○	○
12.	In multiple-function lighting, the key light can act as a back light, and the side light as key, depending on the position of the camera relative to the subject.	12 ○	○
13.	The background light must strike the background from the same side as the key light.	13 ○	○
14.	Color temperature measures the relative reddishness and bluishness of white light.	14 ○	○
15.	The inverse square law applies only if the light source radiates isotropically.	15 ○	○

SECTION TOTAL [   ]

PROBLEM-SOLVING APPLICATIONS

1. You are asked to do the lighting for a shampoo commercial. The director wants you to make the model's blond hair look especially brilliant and glamorous. Which of the three instruments of the lighting triangle needs special attention to achieve the desired result?

2. The show is a brief address by the CEO. Prepare a light plot for the floor plan shown at right. Sketch the type and the locations of the instruments used as well as the general direction of the light beams.

CURTAIN ~~~~~~

TALENT 〇

DESK ▭

3. The assignment editor sends you (the camera operator) and a field reporter to the Plaza Hotel to interview a famous soprano in her room. The field reporter will remain off-camera during the entire interview. The lighting in the hotel room is inadequate, so you need additional lighting. Besides the camera light, you have only one Omni-light at your disposal. Where would you place the Omni-light? Why?

4. You are the LD for an indoor springtime fashion show. The studio audience is seated along both sides of the runway. The novice director suggests low-key lighting to give the show some extra sparkle. Do you agree with the director's suggestion? If so, why? If not, why not? What are your recommendations?

5. You are the LD for a dance number that plays in front of a light-gray cyc. The dancers wear off-white leotards. The choreographer wants them to appear first in cameo as illuminated figures against a dark blue background and then, in one continuous take, as black silhouettes moving against a bright red background. Can you fulfill the choreographer's request? If so, how? If not, why not?

6. You will be shooting an interview with the CEO of a large software company. Her office has a large window without any curtains. How would you light this interview while taking advantage of the daylight coming through the window? List specific lights, their locations, and all necessary support equipment.

7. You are covering the dedication of a new library. It is a cloudless sunny day with the sun reflecting off the brilliant white building. The dedication is planned to happen right in front of the building. What are your concerns regarding lighting? What would you suggest to minimize some of the problems?

8. You are to light a news set in which the two co-anchors (a dark-haired man and a blond woman) sit side-by-side. The man is worried about his wrinkles, especially because his co-anchor has perfectly smooth skin. What lighting would you suggest? Draw a rough light plot that indicates the type and the approximate locations of the instruments used.

12 Video-Recording Procedures and Systems

REVIEW OF KEY TERMS

Match each term with its appropriate definition by filling in the corresponding bubble.

(A) Y/color difference component system
(B) composite system
(C) field log
(D) video leader

(E) lossy compression
(F) codec
(G) sampling
(H) memory card

(I) compression
(J) VR
(K) lossless compression
(L) MPEG-4

1. a codec especially well suited for Internet streaming

1 ○ ○ ○ ○
   A B C D
  ○ ○ ○ ○
   E F G H
  ○ ○ ○ ○
   I J K L

2. a system in which the Y and C signals are combined into a single signal

2 ○ ○ ○ ○
   A B C D
  ○ ○ ○ ○
   E F G H
  ○ ○ ○ ○
   I J K L

3. a recording device that stores and plays back video and audio signals

3 ○ ○ ○ ○
   A B C D
  ○ ○ ○ ○
   E F G H
  ○ ○ ○ ○
   I J K L

PAGE TOTAL [ ]

(A) Y/color difference component system	(E) lossy compression
(B) composite system	(F) codec
(C) field log	(G) sampling
(D) video leader	(H) memory card

(I) compression
(J) VR
(K) lossless compression
(L) MPEG-4

4. selecting equally spaced portions of an analog signal for digitizing

4
- A ○ B ○ C ○ D ○
- E ○ F ○ G ○ H ○
- I ○ J ○ K ○ L ○

5. a read/write solid-state storage device for large amounts of digital data

5
- A ○ B ○ C ○ D ○
- E ○ F ○ G ○ H ○
- I ○ J ○ K ○ L ○

6. standard information recorded ahead of the production footage

6
- A ○ B ○ C ○ D ○
- E ○ F ○ G ○ H ○
- I ○ J ○ K ○ L ○

7. eliminates redundant pixels from each frame

7
- A ○ B ○ C ○ D ○
- E ○ F ○ G ○ H ○
- I ○ J ○ K ○ L ○

8. reduces the amount of digital data for recording or transmission

8
- A ○ B ○ C ○ D ○
- E ○ F ○ G ○ H ○
- I ○ J ○ K ○ L ○

PAGE TOTAL [ ]

9. a list of shots taken during the recording

9　○　○　○　○
　　A　B　C　D
　　○　○　○　○
　　E　F　G　H
　　○　○　○　○
　　I　J　K　L

10. a specific compression standard

10　○　○　○　○
　　A　B　C　D
　　○　○　○　○
　　E　F　G　H
　　○　○　○　○
　　I　J　K　L

11. a system in which the Y signal and the R–Y and B–Y signals are kept separate throughout the video-recording process

11　○　○　○　○
　　A　B　C　D
　　○　○　○　○
　　E　F　G　H
　　○　○　○　○
　　I　J　K　L

12. rearranges pixels for facilitating data storage and transmission.

12　○　○　○　○
　　A　B　C　D
　　○　○　○　○
　　E　F　G　H
　　○　○　○　○
　　I　J　K　L

PAGE
TOTAL　[   ]

SECTION
TOTAL　[   ]

REVIEW OF VIDEO-RECORDING SYSTEMS, SIGNALS, AND CODECS

Select the correct answers and fill in the bubbles with the corresponding letters.

1. Digital recording systems are (A) *nonlinear* (B) *linear* (C) *linear or nonlinear, depending on the recording system.*

   1 ○ A ○ B ○ C

2. The NTSC signal is based on a (A) *Y/C component* (B) *composite* (C) *Y/color difference component* signal.

   2 ○ A ○ B ○ C

3. Disk-based recording systems are always (A) *digital* (B) *analog* (C) *both digital and analog.*

   3 ○ A ○ B ○ C

4. Memory cards (A) *have no moving parts* (B) *can record digital audio only* (C) *can record digital video only.*

   4 ○ A ○ B ○ C

5. The video compression method mostly for still pictures is (A) *MPEG* (B) *JPEG* (C) *RGB.*

   5 ○ A ○ B ○ C

6. The type of compression that looks for redundancies from one frame to the next is (A) *interframe* (B) *intraframe* (C) *lossless.*

   6 ○ A ○ B ○ C

7. A server is a very large-capacity (in the multi-terabyte range) disk array, also called (A) *an SDI* (B) *a RAID* (C) *an SxS.*

   7 ○ A ○ B ○ C

8. The best color fidelity is achieved through a (A) *4:2:2* (B) *4:1:1* (C) *4:0:0* sampling ratio.

   8 ○ A ○ B ○ C

9. The Y/C component signal separates the (A) *color and luminance signals* (B) *audio and video signals* (C) *yellow and cyan color signals.*

   9 ○ A ○ B ○ C

10. The video track of a video leader includes (A) *color bars* (B) *talent credits* (C) *TD's name.*

    10 ○ A ○ B ○ C

11. The clapboard includes (A) *take number* (B) *executive producer* (C) *recording check.*

    11 ○ A ○ B ○ C

12. Intraframe compression eliminates (A) *various frames* (B) *temporal redundancy in each frame* (C) *spatial redundancy in each frame.*

    12 ○ A ○ B ○ C

13. One function that distinguishes a server from a standard large-capacity hard drive is that the server can (A) *record large amounts of digital data* (B) *supply different material to various clients simultaneously* (C) *allow random access of clips.*

    13 ○ A ○ B ○ C

PAGE TOTAL [   ]

14. The advantage of the composite system is that it is one way of saving bandwidth for (A) *an analog color signal* (B) *a digital color signal* (C) *a digital component signal.*

15. The Y/color difference component system (A) *combines the Y and C signals* (B) *separates the Y and C signals* (C) *uses S-video signals* for better video fidelity.

16. The illustration below shows a (A) *Y/C component signal* (B) *Y/color difference component signal* (C) *composite signal.*

Luminance

Color

REVIEW OF VIDEO-RECORDING PROCEDURES

Select the correct answers and fill in the bubbles with the corresponding letters.

1. Because color bars help the video-record operator match the technical aspects of the playback VR and the playback monitor, you should record them (A) *at the beginning of the video recording* (B) *right after the video leader* (C) *at the end of the video recording* for at least (D) *10 seconds* (E) *30 seconds* (F) *5 minutes.* **(Fill in two bubbles.)**

2. The field log is normally kept by the (A) *VR operator* (B) *TD* (C) *VO.*

3. To protect a memory card from being accidentally erased, the small tab (A) *must be in the closed position* (B) *must be in the open position* (C) *cannot prevent erasure.*

4. A media card can record   (A) *only compressed data* (B) *only raw data* (C) *both compressed and raw data.*

5. The clapboard aids in (A) *starting the countdown* (B) *synchronizing audio and video* (C) *marking the first video frame.*

6. Two essential items on a slate or clapboard are (A) *producer and date* (B) *title and take number* (C) *title and executive producer.*

7. The most accurate audio-recording check is to (A) *watch the waveform monitor* (B) *watch the VU meter* (C) *listen through headphones.*

8. The video-recording preparations include (A) *scheduling* (B) *equipment checklist* (C) *keeping a field log.* **(Fill in two bubbles.)**

9. You cannot import clips in a postproduction editing system if it does not recognize the (A) *name* (B) *length* (C) *codec* of the clip.

10. Instead of a clapboard in field production, if necessary you can use (A) *a piece of paper* (B) *verbal slating* (C) *no slate information.*

1	○ A	○ B	○ C
	○ D	○ E	○ F
2	○ A	○ B	○ C
3	○ A	○ B	○ C
4	○ A	○ B	○ C
5	○ A	○ B	○ C
6	○ A	○ B	○ C
7	○ A	○ B	○ C
8	○ A	○ B	○ C
9	○ A	○ B	○ C
10	○ A	○ B	○ C

SECTION TOTAL [ ]

REVIEW QUIZ

*Mark the following statements as true or false by filling in the bubbles in the **T** (for true) or **F** (for false) column.*

		T	F
1.	An advantage of using a memory card for recording is that it has no moving parts.	○	○
2.	You can use the SMPTE time code to mark digital frames.	○	○
3.	In a Y/color difference component system, the Y and R–Y/B–Y signals are kept separate throughout the entire recording process.	○	○
4.	If they are lossy, all codecs are the same.	○	○
5.	You can use a hard disk to record both analog and digital signals.	○	○
6.	Each digital frame has a unique address.	○	○
7.	In the Y/C component system, the color yellow has been added to the color signals.	○	○
8.	You should use prerecorded color bars for the video leader.	○	○
9.	A codec signifies a specific digital compression standard.	○	○
10.	When a camera feeds a switcher in addition to its own VR, it is no longer an iso camera.	○	○
11.	Memory cards and disk-based storage systems allow random access.	○	○
12.	MPEG-2 is a lossless compression technique.	○	○
13.	A 4:2:2 sampling is better than a 4:1:1 sampling.	○	○
14.	Memory cards can store video as well as audio data.	○	○
15.	A *4:1:1* sampling ratio means that the luminance signal is sampled four times as often as each color signal.	○	○

SECTION TOTAL ☐

PROBLEM-SOLVING APPLICATIONS

1. Before purchasing a new camcorder, why should you inquire about the codec it uses for recording?

2. You are asked to produce a brief instructional video on diagnosing specific skin rashes. The physician in charge insists that you use recording equipment that has a 4:2:2 sampling standard. Why is she so insistent about the sampling?

3. Because the extreme conditions under which the digital movie will be shot necessitate extensive audio postproduction and ADR, the editor insists on equipment that uses intraframe rather than interframe compression. Why do you think the editor specifies the compression system?

4. How do intraframe and interframe compression relate to spatial and temporal redundancy?

5. What are the advantages of using memory cards rather than hard drives or optical discs for the camcorder's recording media?

13 Switching, or Instantaneous Editing

REVIEW OF KEY TERMS

Match each term with its appropriate definition by filling in the corresponding bubble.

(A) delegation controls
(B) program bus
(C) key bus
(D) fader bar
(E) preview/preset bus

(F) DSK
(G) switching
(H) genlock
(I) M/E bus

(J) key
(K) auto-transition
(L) super
(M) wipe

1. a lever on a switcher that activates preset functions such as dissolves, fades, and wipes of varying speeds

1 ⃝ ⃝ ⃝ ⃝ ⃝
  A B C D E
  ⃝ ⃝ ⃝ ⃝ ⃝
  F G H I J
  ⃝ ⃝ ⃝
  K L M

2. the bus on a switcher whose inputs are directly switched to the line-out

2 ⃝ ⃝ ⃝ ⃝ ⃝
  A B C D E
  ⃝ ⃝ ⃝ ⃝ ⃝
  F G H I J
  ⃝ ⃝ ⃝
  K L M

3. controls on a switcher that assign specific functions to a bus

3 ⃝ ⃝ ⃝ ⃝ ⃝
  A B C D E
  ⃝ ⃝ ⃝ ⃝ ⃝
  F G H I J
  ⃝ ⃝ ⃝
  K L M

PAGE TOTAL [   ]

(A) delegation controls	(F) DSK	(J) key
(B) program bus	(G) switching	(K) auto-transition
(C) key bus	(H) genlock	(L) super
(D) fader bar	(I) M/E bus	(M) wipe
(E) preview/preset bus		

4. a change from one video source to the next

4

○ ○ ○ ○ ○
A B C D E
○ ○ ○ ○ ○
F G H I J
○ ○ ○
K L M

5. a double exposure of two images

5

○ ○ ○ ○ ○
A B C D E
○ ○ ○ ○ ○
F G H I J
○ ○ ○
K L M

6. electronically cutting letters into a background picture

6

○ ○ ○ ○ ○
A B C D E
○ ○ ○ ○ ○
F G H I J
○ ○ ○
K L M

7. a row of buttons that can serve a mix or an effects function

7

○ ○ ○ ○ ○
A B C D E
○ ○ ○ ○ ○
F G H I J
○ ○ ○
K L M

8. rows of buttons used to select the upcoming video and route it to the preview monitor

8

○ ○ ○ ○ ○
A B C D E
○ ○ ○ ○ ○
F G H I J
○ ○ ○
K L M

P A G E
T O T A L

9. control that allows a title to be keyed over the line-out image as it leaves the switcher

9 ○ ○ ○ ○ ○
   A B C D E
   ○ ○ ○ ○ ○
   F G H I J
   ○ ○ ○
   K L M

10. a bus used to select the video source to be inserted into a background image

10 ○ ○ ○ ○ ○
   A B C D E
   ○ ○ ○ ○ ○
   F G H I J
   ○ ○ ○
   K L M

11. synchronization of video sources or origination sources to prevent picture breakup

11 ○ ○ ○ ○ ○
   A B C D E
   ○ ○ ○ ○ ○
   F G H I J
   ○ ○ ○
   K L M

12. a device that triggers the function of a fader bar

12 ○ ○ ○ ○ ○
   A B C D E
   ○ ○ ○ ○ ○
   F G H I J
   ○ ○ ○
   K L M

13. transition in which the new image is revealed in a pattern or shape

13 ○ ○ ○ ○ ○
   A B C D E
   ○ ○ ○ ○ ○
   F G H I J
   ○ ○ ○
   K L M

PAGE
TOTAL [   ]

SECTION
TOTAL [   ]

REVIEW OF BASIC SWITCHER LAYOUT AND OPERATION

To the instructor: you may want to modify this exercise to show the switcher you are using in your control room.

1. Fill in the bubbles whose letters correspond with the appropriate parts of the switcher shown in the following figure.

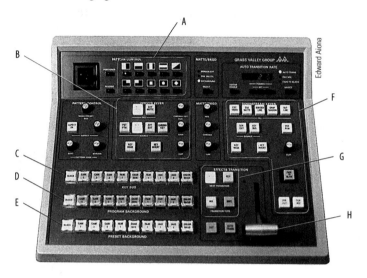

Edward Aiona

a. fader bar

b. preview/preset bus

c. program bus

d. key bus

e. delegation controls (mix/effects transition)

f. wipe pattern selector

g. downstream keyer controls

h. key/matte controls

1a ○ ○ ○ ○
   A B C D
   ○ ○ ○ ○
   E F G H

1b ○ ○ ○ ○
   A B C D
   ○ ○ ○ ○
   E F G H

1c ○ ○ ○ ○
   A B C D
   ○ ○ ○ ○
   E F G H

1d ○ ○ ○ ○
   A B C D
   ○ ○ ○ ○
   E F G H

1e ○ ○ ○ ○
   A B C D
   ○ ○ ○ ○
   E F G H

1f ○ ○ ○ ○
   A B C D
   ○ ○ ○ ○
   E F G H

1g ○ ○ ○ ○
   A B C D
   ○ ○ ○ ○
   E F G H

1h ○ ○ ○ ○
   A B C D
   ○ ○ ○ ○
   E F G H

PAGE
TOTAL

Select the correct answers and fill in the bubbles with the corresponding letters.

2. To have C3 (camera 3) appear on the preview monitor before switching to it from C1, you need to (A) *press C3 on the preview bus* (B) *press C3 on the preview bus, then press the key button* (C) *press C3 on the program bus, then move the fader bar to the opposite position.*

    2 ◯ A ◯ B ◯ C

3. Assuming that the final credits are keyed with the DSK, you can go to black by (A) *pressing the black button on the program bus* (B) *pressing the black button on the key bus* (C) *pressing the black button in the downstream keyer section.*

    3 ◯ A ◯ B ◯ C

4. To dissolve from C3 to VR (with the auto-transition in the *off* position), you (A) *press the VR button on the preview bus; then press the cut button* (B) *press the VR button on the preview bus; then move the fader bar to the opposite position* (C) *press the VR button on the key bus; then move the fader bar to the opposite position.*

    4 ◯ A ◯ B ◯ C

5. To select the functions of a specific bus or buses, you need to activate the (A) *key-level control* (B) *wipe mode selectors* (C) *delegation controls.*

    5 ◯ A ◯ B ◯ C

6. To switch from C1 to C3 by pressing only one button, you need to press the (A) *C3 button on the preview bus* (B) *C3 button on the key bus* (C) *C3 button on the program bus.* **(This assumes that the appropriate buses have already been delegated a mix/effects function.)**

    6 ◯ A ◯ B ◯ C

7. The program bus will direct the selected video source to the (A) *preview monitor* (B) *mix bus* (C) *line-out.*

    7 ◯ A ◯ B ◯ C

8. When switching repeatedly from one person to another during an O/S sequence, it is best to use the (A) *fader bar* (B) *cut button* (C) *mix button.*

    8 ◯ A ◯ B ◯ C

9. The speed of an automated transition is determined by (A) *how fast you move the fader bar* (B) *the time you dial into the auto-transition* (C) *how fast you switch on the program bus.*

    9 ◯ A ◯ B ◯ C

P A G E
T O T A L

10. Identify the proper preview and line monitor images you would expect to see from the switcher output and fill in the corresponding bubble. The highlighted buttons on the following switcher have already been pressed. C1 is focused on the host, C2 on the dancers (see the monitor images below).

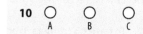

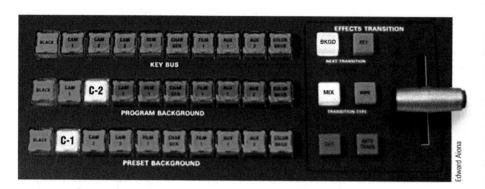

A

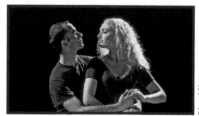

Preview

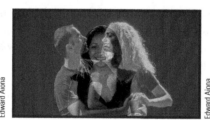

Line

B

Preview

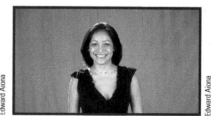

Line

C

Preview

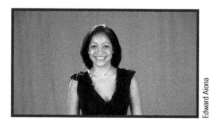

Line

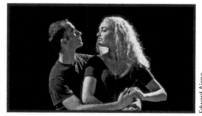

PAGE
TOTAL

11. Identify the proper preview and line monitor images you would expect to see from the switcher output by filling in the corresponding bubble.

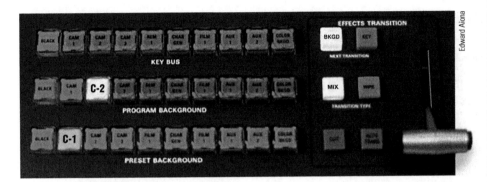

A

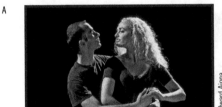

Preview

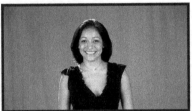

Line

B

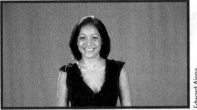

Preview

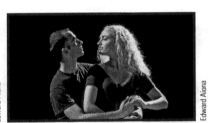

Line

C

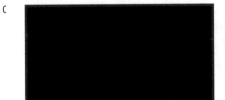

Preview

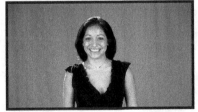

Line

12. Identify the proper preview and line monitor images you would expect to see from the switcher output at the end of the previous dissolve and fill in the corresponding bubble.

12 ○ ○ ○
   A   B   C

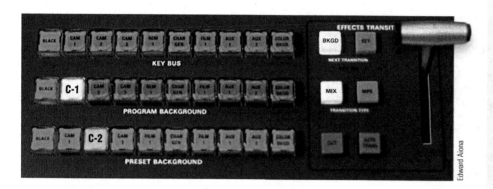

Edward Aiona

A

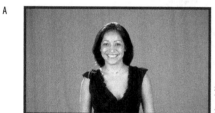

Preview

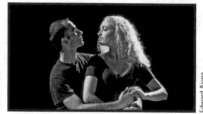

Line

Edward Aiona

B

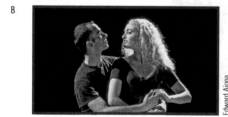

Preview

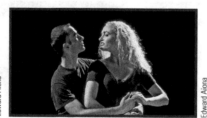

Line

Edward Aiona

C

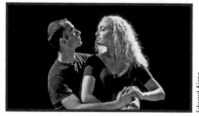

Preview

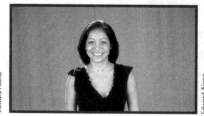

Line

Edward Aiona

REVIEW QUIZ

*Mark the following statements as true or false by filling in the bubbles in the **T** (for true) or **F** (for false) column.*

		T	F
1.	Through delegation controls, you can assign a preview function to the program bus.	**1** ○	○
2.	The downstream keyer can add a title key only if there are no other keys present in the line-out picture.	**2** ○	○
3.	Electronically cutting out portions of a background image and filling them with color is called a superimposition.	**3** ○	○
4.	The auto-transition fulfills the same function as the fader bar.	**4** ○	○
5.	The switcher has a separate button for each video input.	**5** ○	○
6.	Assuming that the DSK is inactive, the black button from the program bus will put the line into black.	**6** ○	○
7.	The preview bus can also be used as a mix bus, if so delegated.	**7** ○	○
8.	Assuming that you are not using auto-transition, the speed of a dissolve depends on how fast the fader bar is moved up or down.	**8** ○	○
9.	The DSK black button will put the switcher output to black regardless of what source feeds the line-out.	**9** ○	○
10.	It is impossible to have both preset and program buses activated at the same time.	**10** ○	○
11.	The cut button will switch between the video sources that are preset on the program bus.	**11** ○	○

SECTION
TOTAL

PROBLEM-SOLVING APPLICATIONS

1. The director asks you, the TD, to superimpose a long shot of a dancer over a close-up of her face. The director wants to first have the long shot be the more prominent image and then slowly shift the emphasis to the close-up. How, if at all, can you accomplish such an effect?

2. The director wants you to perform four dissolves that are identical in speed from one dancer to the next. Are such identical dissolves possible? If so, how can they be accomplished? If not, why not?

3. You have keyed the credits over the base picture with the downstream keyer. When the director calls for a fade to black, you press the black button on the program bus. What will you see on the line monitor? Why?

4. The director wants you to do fast cuts between the CUs of the interviewer and the guest during a lively discussion. How can you best accomplish such fast cuts between the two?

5. When you, the TD, preview the key of a CG title, the white letters tear at the edges. How can you correct this problem?

14 Design

REVIEW OF KEY TERMS

Match each term with its appropriate definition by filling in the corresponding bubble.

(A) letterbox
(B) grayscale
(C) pillarbox
(D) virtual set
(E) floor plan

(F) additive primary colors
(G) essential area
(H) scanning area
(I) saturation
(J) aspect ratio

(K) props
(L) windowbox
(M) color compatibility
(N) branding

1. the picture area usually seen on the camera viewfinder and the preview monitor

1
○ ○ ○ ○ ○
A B C D E
○ ○ ○ ○ ○
F G H I J
○ ○ ○ ○
K L M N

2. furniture and other objects used for set decorations or by actors or performers

2
○ ○ ○ ○ ○
A B C D E
○ ○ ○ ○ ○
F G H I J
○ ○ ○ ○
K L M N

3. colors with enough brightness contrast for good monochrome reproduction

3
○ ○ ○ ○ ○
A B C D E
○ ○ ○ ○ ○
F G H I J
○ ○ ○ ○
K L M N

PAGE TOTAL [   ]

(A) letterbox	(F) additive primary colors	(K) props
(B) grayscale	(G) essential area	(L) windowbox
(C) pillarbox	(H) scanning area	(M) color compatibility
(D) virtual set	(I) saturation	(N) branding
(E) floor plan	(J) aspect ratio	

4. the width-to-height proportions of the video screen

4
A B C D E
F G H I J
K L M N

5. the section of the television picture, centered within the scanning area, that the home viewer sees

5
A B C D E
F G H I J
K L M N

6. fitting a 16 × 9 aspect ratio into a 4 × 3 screen without cropping or distortion

6
A B C D E
F G H I J
K L M N

7. the color attribute that describes a color's richness or strength

7
A B C D E
F G H I J
K L M N

8. a smaller frame positioned in the center of the TV screen

8
A B C D E
F G H I J
K L M N

PAGE TOTAL

9. a measure of the intermediate steps from TV white to TV black

9 ◯ ◯ ◯ ◯ ◯
A B C D E
◯ ◯ ◯ ◯ ◯
F G H I J
◯ ◯ ◯ ◯
K L M N

10. a diagram of scenery and major set properties drawn on a grid

10 ◯ ◯ ◯ ◯ ◯
A B C D E
◯ ◯ ◯ ◯ ◯
F G H I J
◯ ◯ ◯ ◯
K L M N

11. fitting a 4 × 3 aspect ratio into a 16 × 9 screen without cropping or distortion

11 ◯ ◯ ◯ ◯ ◯
A B C D E
◯ ◯ ◯ ◯ ◯
F G H I J
◯ ◯ ◯ ◯
K L M N

12. red, green, and blue

12 ◯ ◯ ◯ ◯ ◯
A B C D E
◯ ◯ ◯ ◯ ◯
F G H I J
◯ ◯ ◯ ◯
K L M N

13. a computer-generated environment

13 ◯ ◯ ◯ ◯ ◯
A B C D E
◯ ◯ ◯ ◯ ◯
F G H I J
◯ ◯ ◯ ◯
K L M N

14. establishing a station identity to attract and retain loyal viewers

14 ◯ ◯ ◯ ◯ ◯
A B C D E
◯ ◯ ◯ ◯ ◯
F G H I J
◯ ◯ ◯ ◯
K L M N

PAGE TOTAL [ ]

SECTION TOTAL [ ]

REVIEW OF TELEVISION GRAPHICS

Select the correct answers and fill in the bubbles with the corresponding letters.

1. The standard television aspect ratio is (A) *4 × 3* (B) *8 × 12* (C) *16 × 9*. For HDTV it is (D) *4 × 3* (E) *8 × 12* (F) *16 × 9*. **(Fill in two bubbles.)**

2. All lettering must be contained within the (A) *scanning area* (B) *screen area* (C) *essential area.*

3. The color attribute that determines how dark or light a color appears on the monochrome television screen is (A) *hue* (B) *brightness* (C) *saturation.*

4. On a grayscale *1* represents (A) *TV white* (B) *TV black* (C) *100 percent reflectance.*

5. *Color compatibility* refers to using colors that differ distinctly as to (A) *hue* (B) *saturation* (C) *brightness.*

6. The image generator built into the switcher that produces special-effects wipe patterns and keys is the (A) *DVE* (B) *SEG* (C) *CG.*

7. The aesthetic energy of a color is principally determined by (A) *hue and saturation* (B) *the color itself* (C) *brightness and saturation.*

8. To store a great many titles for instant access, you need (A) *a CG* (B) *DVE* (C) *an SEG.*

9. Normally, low-energy colors are used more for the (A) *foreground* (B) *middleground* (C) *background* in a scene.

10. Dead zones are (A) *uninteresting picture areas* (B) *the empty vertical bars when showing standard TV on HDTV* (C) *a sound problem in studio areas.*

11. The whiteboard writing shown in the photo below is (A) *appropriate* (B) *inappropriate* because it (C) *is within the scanning area* (D) *does not permit good CUs.*
    (Fill in two bubbles.)

1	○ A	○ B	○ C
	○ D	○ E	○ F
2	○ A	○ B	○ C
3	○ A	○ B	○ C
4	○ A	○ B	○ C
5	○ A	○ B	○ C
6	○ A	○ B	○ C
7	○ A	○ B	○ C
8	○ A	○ B	○ C
9	○ A	○ B	○ C
10	○ A	○ B	○ C
11	○ A	○ B	
	○ C	○ D	

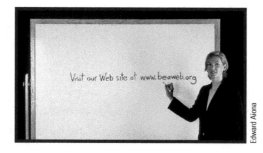

Edward Aiona

PAGE TOTAL

12. The following six figures show various television graphics displayed on well-adjusted preview monitors. These monitors show the entire scanning area. For each figure state whether you would (A) *accept* (B) *not accept* the television graphic because it has (C) *inappropriate style* (D) *enough contrast between figure and ground* (E) *scattered information* (F) *good grouping of words* (G) *letters that are too small* (H) *information that lies outside the essential area* (I) *letters that get lost in the busy background*.
(Fill in the two bubbles that seem most appropriate for each graphic.)

Zoom control ring

Focus ring   Iris control ring

a.

Nuclear Crisis

b.

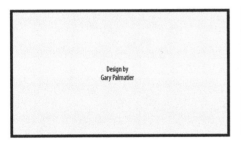

Design by
Gary Palmatier

c.

Dancers:
Stephanie Ream
Nicole Beynon
Florence Holsted
Jane Frost

d.

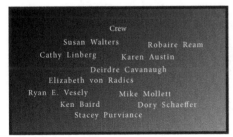

Crew
Susan Walters   Robaire Ream
Cathy Linberg   Karen Austin
        Deirdre Cavanaugh
    Elizabeth von Radics
Ryan E. Vesely   Mike Mollett
    Ken Baird   Dory Schaeffer
        Stacey Purviance

e.

EARTHQUAKE

Herbert Zettl

f.

12a ○A ○B
     ○C ○D ○E ○F
     ○G ○H ○I

12b ○A ○B
     ○C ○D ○E ○F
     ○G ○H ○I

12c ○A ○B
     ○C ○D ○E ○F
     ○G ○H ○I

12d ○A ○B
     ○C ○D ○E ○F
     ○G ○H ○I

12e ○A ○B
     ○C ○D ○E ○F
     ○G ○H ○I

12f ○A ○B
     ○C ○D ○E ○F
     ○G ○H ○I

PAGE TOTAL

13. Fill in the bubbles whose letters correspond with the appropriate title areas in the following figure.

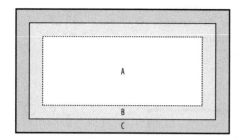

a. total graphic screen area

b. essential area

c. scanning area

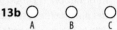

13a ⭘ A   ⭘ B   ⭘ C

13b ⭘ A   ⭘ B   ⭘ C

13c ⭘ A   ⭘ B   ⭘ C

14. The color attribute that is the color itself is (A) *hue* (B) *brightness* (C) *saturation.*

14 ⭘ A   ⭘ B   ⭘ C

15. The vertically oriented diagram below is (A) *acceptable* (B) *not acceptable* for shooting with a studio camera because (C) *it is not in proper aspect ratio* (D) *the camera can tilt in a close-up.* **(Fill in two bubbles.)**

15 ⭘ A   ⭘ B

   ⭘ C   ⭘ D

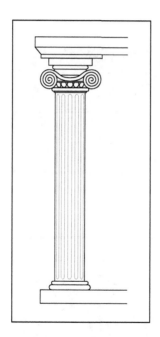

PAGE
TOTAL

16. Fill in the bubbles whose letters correspond with the type of digital distortion that results from adjusting one aspect ratio to fit another.

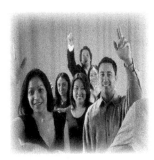 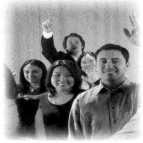

Edward Aiona

A   B

    a. a 4 × 3 shot viewed full-screen on a 16 × 9 monitor

    16a ◯ A   ◯ B

    b. a 16 × 9 shot viewed full-screen on a 4 × 3 monitor

    16b ◯ A   ◯ B

17. Fill in the bubbles whose letters correspond with the appropriate aspect ratio or frame adjustments in the figure.

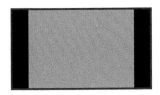 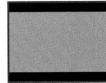 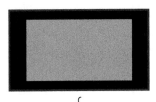

A   B   C

    a. windowbox

    17a ◯ A   ◯ B   ◯ C

    b. pillarbox

    17b ◯ A   ◯ B   ◯ C

    c. letterbox

    17c ◯ A   ◯ B   ◯ C

18. RGB colored lights combined in various proportions to produce all other colors is known as (A) *subtractive color mixing* (B) *additive color mixing* (C) *primary colors of light.*

    18 ◯ A   ◯ B   ◯ C

PAGE TOTAL [   ]

SECTION TOTAL [   ]

REVIEW OF SCENERY AND SCENIC DESIGN

Select the correct answers and fill in the bubbles with the corresponding letters.

1. The continuous piece of canvas or muslin along two, three, or even all four studio walls to form a uniform background is referred to as (A) *a drop* (B) *canvas backing* (C) *a cyclorama.*

2. To elevate scenery, properties, or action areas, we use (A) *periaktoi* (B) *platforms* (C) *pylons.*

3. The standard backgrounds to simulate interior and exterior walls are called (A) *cycs* (B) *flats* (C) *drops.*

4. The usual height for standard set units is (A) *7 feet* (B) *10 feet* (C) *14 feet.* For studios with low ceilings, it is (D) *6 feet* (E) *8 feet* (F) *12 feet.* **(Fill in two bubbles.)**

5. Pictures and draperies are (A) *set dressings* (B) *set decorations* (C) *hand props.*

1 ○ A   ○ B   ○ C

2 ○ A   ○ B   ○ C

3 ○ A   ○ B   ○ C

4 ○ A   ○ B   ○ C
   ○ D   ○ E   ○ F

5 ○ A   ○ B   ○ C

PAGE
TOTAL

6. Fill in the bubbles whose letters correspond with the letters identifying the various set pieces shown below.

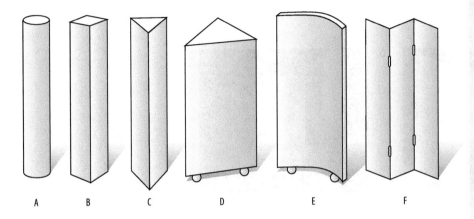

A   B   C   D   E   F

a. periaktos

b. round pillar

c. sweep

d. screen

e. pylon

f. square pillar

	A	B	C	D	E	F
6a	○	○	○	○	○	○
6b	○	○	○	○	○	○
6c	○	○	○	○	○	○
6d	○	○	○	○	○	○
6e	○	○	○	○	○	○
6f	○	○	○	○	○	○

PAGE TOTAL [ ]

7. For the simple sets shown below, select the floor plan shown on the facing page that most closely corresponds and fill in the appropriate bubbles. *(Assume that the camera shoots straight-on. Note that there are floor plans that do not match any of the set photos. The floor plans are not to scale.)*

a.
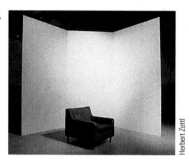
Herbert Zettl

b.
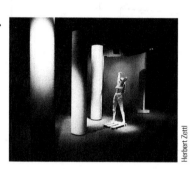
Herbert Zettl

c.
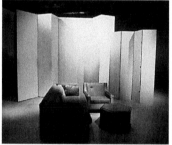
Herbert Zettl

d.
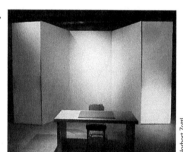
Herbert Zettl

e.
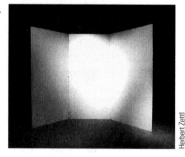
Herbert Zettl

f.
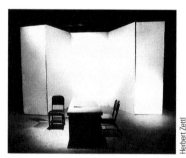
Herbert Zettl

7a ⓐ Ⓐ Ⓑ Ⓒ Ⓓ Ⓔ
   A B C D E
   Ⓕ Ⓖ Ⓗ Ⓘ
   F G H I

7b Ⓐ Ⓑ Ⓒ Ⓓ Ⓔ
   A B C D E
   Ⓕ Ⓖ Ⓗ Ⓘ
   F G H I

7c Ⓐ Ⓑ Ⓒ Ⓓ Ⓔ
   A B C D E
   Ⓕ Ⓖ Ⓗ Ⓘ
   F G H I

7d Ⓐ Ⓑ Ⓒ Ⓓ Ⓔ
   A B C D E
   Ⓕ Ⓖ Ⓗ Ⓘ
   F G H I

7e Ⓐ Ⓑ Ⓒ Ⓓ Ⓔ
   A B C D E
   Ⓕ Ⓖ Ⓗ Ⓘ
   F G H I

7f Ⓐ Ⓑ Ⓒ Ⓓ Ⓔ
   A B C D E
   Ⓕ Ⓖ Ⓗ Ⓘ
   F G H I

PAGE
TOTAL

SECTION
TOTAL

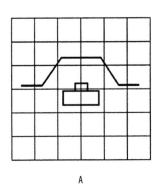

A

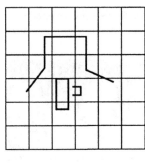

B

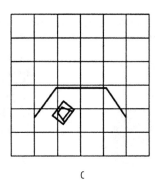

C

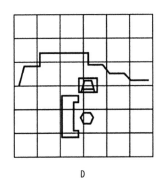

D

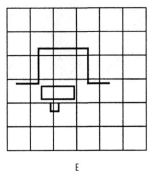

E

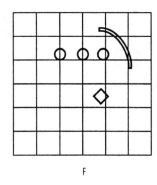

F

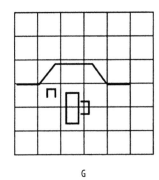

G

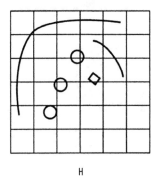

H

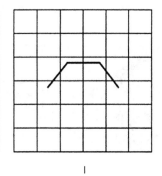

I

REVIEW OF ELECTRONIC EFFECTS

1. Fill in the bubbles whose numbers correspond with the appropriate electronic effects illustrated in the following figures.

A
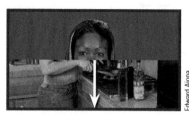
Edward Aiona

B
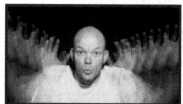
Edward Aiona

C
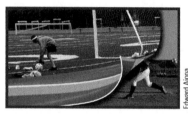
Edward Aiona

D
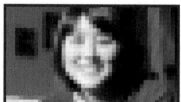
Edward Aiona

E
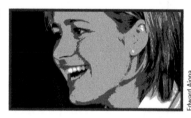
Edward Aiona

F
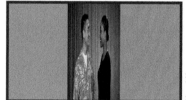
Edward Aiona

G
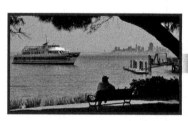
Edward Aiona

H
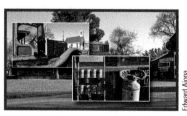
Edward Aiona

I
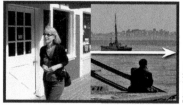
Edward Aiona

a. echo effect

1a ◯ ◯ ◯ ◯ ◯
    A   B   C   D   E
◯ ◯ ◯ ◯
F   G   H   I

b. vertical wipe

1b ◯ ◯ ◯ ◯ ◯
    A   B   C   D   E
◯ ◯ ◯ ◯
F   G   H   I

c. multiple frames

1c ◯ ◯ ◯ ◯ ◯
    A   B   C   D   E
◯ ◯ ◯ ◯
F   G   H   I

d. shrinking effect

1d ◯ ◯ ◯ ◯ ◯
    A   B   C   D   E
◯ ◯ ◯ ◯
F   G   H   I

e. mosaic effect

1e ◯ ◯ ◯ ◯ ◯
    A   B   C   D   E
◯ ◯ ◯ ◯
F   G   H   I

f. peel effect

1f ◯ ◯ ◯ ◯ ◯
    A   B   C   D   E
◯ ◯ ◯ ◯
F   G   H   I

g. vertical stretching

1g ◯ ◯ ◯ ◯ ◯
    A   B   C   D   E
◯ ◯ ◯ ◯
F   G   H   I

h. horizontal wipe

1h ◯ ◯ ◯ ◯ ◯
    A   B   C   D   E
◯ ◯ ◯ ◯
F   G   H   I

i. posterization

1i ◯ ◯ ◯ ◯ ◯
    A   B   C   D   E
◯ ◯ ◯ ◯
F   G   H   I

SECTION TOTAL [ ]

REVIEW QUIZ

*Mark the following statements as true or false by filling in the bubbles in the **T** (for true) or **F** (for false) column.*

		T	F
1.	Screen clutter can be avoided by grouping related information in specific screen areas.	○	○
2.	So long as there are distinct colors, brightness differences are relatively unimportant in digital cinema.	○	○
3.	Displaying the television station logo on the screen throughout the program is known as windowboxing.	○	○
4.	A floor plan must show the location of flats but can omit the set properties.	○	○
5.	Hardwall scenery is preferred for permanent sets.	○	○
6.	There is an inevitable picture loss when wide-screen movies are shown in their true aspect ratio on a traditional (4 x 3) television screen.	○	○
7.	The scanning area is contained within the essential area.	○	○
8.	Distinctly different hues (such as red and green) guarantee good brightness contrast.	○	○
9.	Pillarboxing is used to fit a 4×3 aspect ratio into a 16×9 screen without distortion.	○	○
10.	A good floor plan will aid the LD in the lighting design.	○	○
11.	The energy of a color is determined primarily by hue.	○	○
12.	For normal screen titles, all written information must extend beyond the scanning area.	○	○
13.	Bold lettering is especially important for mobile media displays.	○	○
14.	Digitally stretching a 4×3 scene to fill a 16×9 screen will make the people in it appear fat.	○	○
15.	In additive color mixing, red and green produce yellow.	○	○
16.	High-energy colors are best displayed against a high-energy-color background.	○	○
17.	A split screen is achieved by stopping a wipe midway in its horizontal travel.	○	○
18.	Shrinking effects differ from box wipes in that they maintain the total picture area and aspect ratio during the reduction.	○	○

SECTION TOTAL [   ]

PROBLEM-SOLVING APPLICATIONS

1. You are asked to direct a variety of shows and evaluate the location sketch or floor plans (see **a** through **c**). Please be specific as to the potential problems in scale (sets and props), camera accessibility and acceptable shots, lighting, and talent traffic.

   a. This location sketch shows the office of the CEO, who would like to make her monthly 4 p.m. live-satellite TV report from behind her desk.

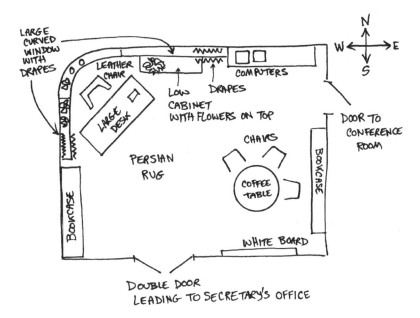

   b. Here is a floor plan for a two-camera live-recorded production of a panel discussion by six prominent businesspeople and a moderator.

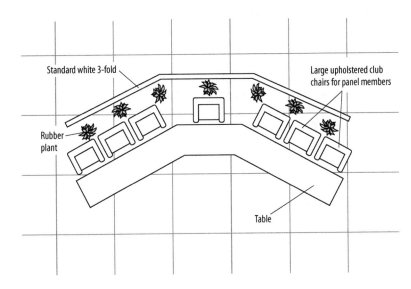

c. This floor plan is for a two-camera live interview set for a morning show.

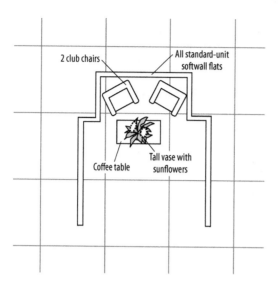

2 club chairs

All standard-unit softwall flats

Tall vase with sunflowers

Coffee table

2. Draw a floor plan for a weekly interview show dealing with the art and media scene in your city. The host will interview guests from stage, screen, and radio. Include a detailed prop list. (Use one of the floor plan patterns provided at the back of this book.)

3. Draw a floor plan for a morning news set. The anchors are a woman and a man, and the news content is geared more toward local gossip than international politics. (Use one of the floor plan patterns provided at the back of this book.)

4. The general manager of your corporation would like you to use a highly detailed photo of the latest computer design as the background for the opening and closing titles. Can you accommodate the request and still make the titles optimally readable?

5. The art director proudly shows you the dancing Chinese-like lettering he has created with his titling software for the name identification of the new Chinese consul. Would you use such a title key? If so, why? If not, why not?

6. The AD informs you, the director, that a dancer who is supposed to be chroma-keyed over a video-recorded landscape scene is wearing a saturated blue leotard. The AD is very concerned about this, but the TD assures you that she has already taken care of the problem. What was the potential problem? How did the TD solve it?

7. The novice news director would like you, the director, to use a circle wipe to close each story. How do you respond? Why?

8. The same director suggests peel effects between the stories of a headline news teaser. How do you respond? Why?

15 Television Talent

REVIEW OF KEY TERMS

Match each term with its appropriate definition by filling in the corresponding bubble.

(A) performer   (D) cue card   (G) blocking
(B) teleprompter   (E) cake   (H) talent
(C) actor   (F) makeup

1. carefully worked-out position, movement, and actions by the talent

   1 ○ ○ ○ ○
      A B C D
      ○ ○ ○ ○
      E F G H

2. a person who appears on-camera in a nondramatic role

   2 ○ ○ ○ ○
      A B C D
      ○ ○ ○ ○
      E F G H

3. a person who appears on-camera in a dramatic role

   3 ○ ○ ○ ○
      A B C D
      ○ ○ ○ ○
      E F G H

4. a large, hand-lettered posterboard that contains on-air copy

   4 ○ ○ ○ ○
      A B C D
      ○ ○ ○ ○
      E F G H

PAGE
TOTAL [   ]

(A) performer	(D) cue card	(G) blocking
(B) teleprompter	(E) cake	(H) talent
(C) actor	(F) makeup	

5. all people who regularly appear on television

5
A ○ B ○ C ○ D ○
E ○ F ○ G ○ H ○

6. cosmetics used to enhance, correct, or change appearance

6
A ○ B ○ C ○ D ○
E ○ F ○ G ○ H ○

7. water-soluble foundation makeup

7
A ○ B ○ C ○ D ○
E ○ F ○ G ○ H ○

8. also known as auto-cue

8
A ○ B ○ C ○ D ○
E ○ F ○ G ○ H ○

PAGE TOTAL

SECTION TOTAL

REVIEW OF PERFORMANCE TECHNIQUES

1. The following pictures show various *time* cues given to the talent by the floor manager. From the list below, select the specific cue illustrated and fill in the bubble with the corresponding letter.

(A) 5 minutes left   (E) stretch   (H) standby
(B) 30 seconds left   (F) cut   (I) cue
(C) 15 seconds left   (G) wind up   (J) speed up
(D) on time

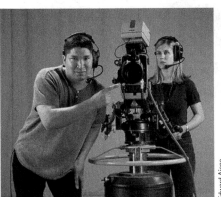

a.

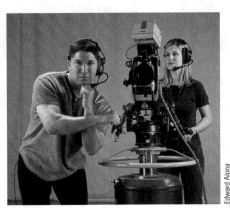

b.

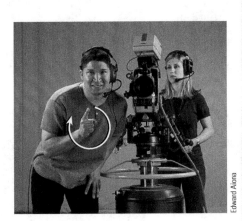

c.   d.

1a ◯ ◯ ◯ ◯ ◯
    A B C D E
    ◯ ◯ ◯ ◯ ◯
    F G H I J

1b ◯ ◯ ◯ ◯ ◯
    A B C D E
    ◯ ◯ ◯ ◯ ◯
    F G H I J

1c ◯ ◯ ◯ ◯ ◯
    A B C D E
    ◯ ◯ ◯ ◯ ◯
    F G H I J

1d ◯ ◯ ◯ ◯ ◯
    A B C D E
    ◯ ◯ ◯ ◯ ◯
    F G H I J

P A G E
T O T A L

(A)	5 minutes left	(E)	stretch	(H)	standby
(B)	30 seconds left	(F)	cut	(I)	cue
(C)	15 seconds left	(G)	wind up	(J)	speed up
(D)	on time				

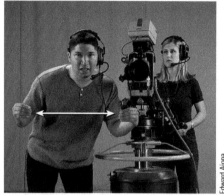

e.

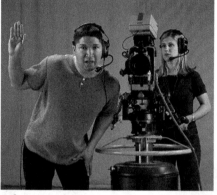

f.

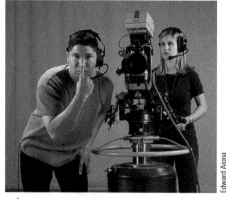

g.

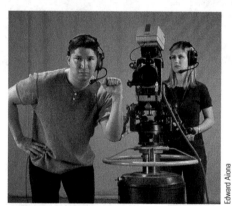

h.

i.

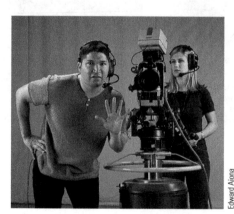

j.

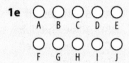

1e A B C D E   F G H I J

1f A B C D E   F G H I J

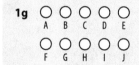

1g A B C D E   F G H I J

1h A B C D E   F G H I J

1i A B C D E   F G H I J

1j A B C D E   F G H I J

P A G E
T O T A L

2. The following pictures show various *directional* and *audio* cues given to the talent by the floor manager. From the list below, select the specific cue illustrated and fill in the bubble with the corresponding letter.

(A) tone down
(B) back
(C) speak up

(D) closer
(E) OK
(F) closer to mic

(G) keep talking
(H) walk

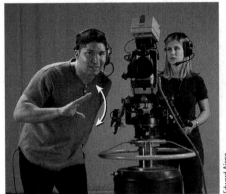

a.

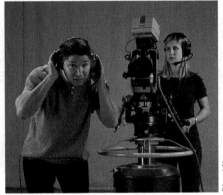

b.

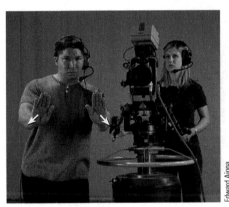

c.

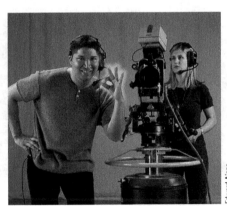

d.

2a
○ ○ ○ ○
A B C D
○ ○ ○ ○
E F G H

2b
○ ○ ○ ○
A B C D
○ ○ ○ ○
E F G H

2c
○ ○ ○ ○
A B C D
○ ○ ○ ○
E F G H

2d
○ ○ ○ ○
A B C D
○ ○ ○ ○
E F G H

P A G E
T O T A L

(A)	tone down	(D)	closer	(G)	keep talking
(B)	back	(E)	OK	(H)	walk
(C)	speak up	(F)	closer to mic		

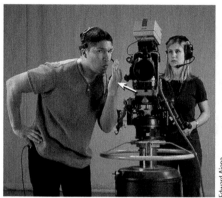

e.

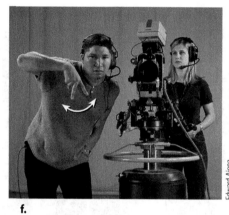

f.

2e ○ ○ ○ ○
    A B C D
    ○ ○ ○ ○
    E F G H

2f ○ ○ ○ ○
    A B C D
    ○ ○ ○ ○
    E F G H

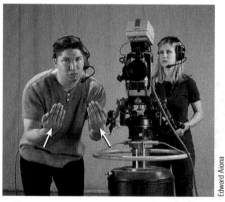

g.

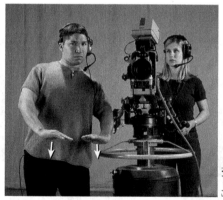

h.

2g ○ ○ ○ ○
    A B C D
    ○ ○ ○ ○
    E F G H

2h ○ ○ ○ ○
    A B C D
    ○ ○ ○ ○
    E F G H

PAGE TOTAL

Edward Aiona

3. From the list below, select the microphone most appropriate for the various performance and acting tasks and fill in the bubbles with the corresponding letters.

(A) fishpole mic
(B) wireless lavalier mic
(C) stand mic

(D) lavalier mic
(E) hand mic
(F) desk mic

(G) wireless hand mic
(H) boom mic

a. lead guitarist with a rock band, who also sings and talks to the audience from the stage

3a ○ ○ ○ ○
   A B C D
   ○ ○ ○ ○
   E F G H

b. two actors doing an outdoor scene

3b ○ ○ ○ ○
   A B C D
   ○ ○ ○ ○
   E F G H

c. singer who is also doing brief dance steps, accompanied by a large band

3c ○ ○ ○ ○
   A B C D
   ○ ○ ○ ○
   E F G H

d. news anchors who remain seated throughout a studio newscast

3d ○ ○ ○ ○
   A B C D
   ○ ○ ○ ○
   E F G H

e. moderating a panel discussion with six people

3e ○ ○ ○ ○
   A B C D
   ○ ○ ○ ○
   E F G H

f. multiple-camera O/S shots involving two actors in a soap opera

3f ○ ○ ○ ○
   A B C D
   ○ ○ ○ ○
   E F G H

g. sounds of breathing and skis on snow during a downhill race

3g ○ ○ ○ ○
   A B C D
   ○ ○ ○ ○
   E F G H

h. interview with a celebrity at a busy airport gate

3h ○ ○ ○ ○
   A B C D
   ○ ○ ○ ○
   E F G H

P A G E
T O T A L [ ]

Select the correct answers and fill in the bubbles with the corresponding letters.

4. When wearing a lavalier mic, you should (A) *maintain your voice level regardless of how far the camera is from you* (B) *increase your volume when the camera gets farther away from you* (C) *speak more softly when the camera is relatively close to you.*

4 ○ A   ○ B   ○ C

5. When making an on-camera announcement in the studio, you should normally take your opening cue from the (A) *camera tally light* (B) *camera operator* (C) *floor manager.*

5 ○ A   ○ B   ○ C

6. When you notice that you are looking into the wrong (not switched on-the-air) camera, you should (A) *look down and then up again into the on-the-air camera* (B) *glance immediately over to the on-the-air camera* (C) *keep looking into the wrong camera until it is punched up on the air.*

6 ○ A   ○ B   ○ C

7. For the talent the most accurate indicator of the camera's field of view is the (A) *relative distance between talent and camera* (B) *floor manager's cues* (C) *studio monitor.*

7 ○ A   ○ B   ○ C

8. When asked for an audio level, you should (A) *quickly count to 10* (B) *say one sentence with a slightly lower voice than when on the air* (C) *speak with your on-the-air voice until told that the level has been taken.*

8 ○ A   ○ B   ○ C

9. When demonstrating a product during a two-camera live show, you should orient the product toward the (A) *close-up camera* (B) *medium-shot camera* and keep looking at the (C) *close-up camera* (D) *medium-shot camera.* **(Fill in two bubbles.)**

9 ○ A   ○ B
   ○ C   ○ D

10. When you receive cues during the actual video-recording that differ from the rehearsed ones, you should (A) *execute the action as rehearsed* (B) *follow the floor manager's cues* (C) *check with the director.*

10 ○ A   ○ B   ○ C

11. When demonstrating a small object, you should (A) *hold it as close to the lens as possible* (B) *keep it as steady as possible on the display table* (C) *lift it up for optimal camera pickup.*

11 ○ A   ○ B   ○ C

PAGE
TOTAL

SECTION
TOTAL

REVIEW OF ACTING TECHNIQUES

Select the correct answers and fill in the bubbles with the corresponding letters.

1. When on a close-up, you should (A) *slow down* (B) *accelerate* (C) *not change* the speed of your on-camera actions.

2. When the camera is relatively far away from you, you should (A) *exaggerate your facial expressions* (B) *exaggerate your gestures* (C) *maintain your close-up acting style.*

3. A "blocking map" is (A) *a rough map drawn by the floor manager* (B) *a mental map to remember prominent positions* (C) *the lines drawn on the floor by the AD.*

4. When blocked in the camera-far position in an O/S shot, you must make sure that you can see the (A) *tally light* (B) *floor manager* (C) *camera lens.*

5. When acting for television, you should project your motions and emotions as you would on the stage (A) *when there is a prolonged dialogue pause* (B) *never* (C) *every time the camera is relatively far away.*

6. Television plays are video-recorded (A) *in the order of scenes from the beginning to the end of the script* (B) *in brief scenes, grouped by location, characters involved, and so forth* (C) *according to the mood of the director.*

7. In a standard studio-recorded daytime serial, the television camera looks at you primarily in (A) *long shots* (B) *close-ups* (C) *low-level shots.*

8. After the blocking rehearsal with the director, you (A) *can make minor changes if the camera operator concurs* (B) *must keep the exact blocking as rehearsed* (C) *can suggest a different blocking during the video-recording.*

9. When auditioning for a television drama, you should (A) *apply your theatre technique to show that you have stage training* (B) *wear something unusual so the director will remember you* (C) *internalize the role as much as possible.*

10. When repeating action for close-ups (such as drinking a glass of milk), you (A) *use the opportunity to improve on what you have done in the long or medium shots* (B) *get a new glass and have it refilled for each close-up* (C) *use the same props and have your glass filled to the level just before the close-up.*

#	A	B	C
1	O	O	O
2	O	O	O
3	O	O	O
4	O	O	O
5	O	O	O
6	O	O	O
7	O	O	O
8	O	O	O
9	O	O	O
10	O	O	O

SECTION TOTAL [ ]

REVIEW OF MAKEUP AND CLOTHING

Select the correct answers and fill in the bubbles with the corresponding letters.

1. One of the most widely used makeup foundations is (A) *cake* (B) *grease base* (C) *pan-stick.*

2. Clothing with thin, highly contrasting stripes or checkered patterns is (A) *acceptable* (B) *not acceptable* because (C) *the digital camera CCD can handle such a contrast* (D) *it provides exciting patterns* (E) *it causes moiré color vibrations* (F) *it is too detailed for the camera to see.* **(Fill in two bubbles.)**

3. The dress of a pop singer has many rhinestones that sparkle under the colored stage lights. This dress is (A) *acceptable* (B) *not acceptable* because (C) *the color camera can handle small areas of bright light* (D) *there is too much brightness contrast* (E) *it will cause moiré patterns* (F) *it will help raise the baselight level.* **(Fill in two bubbles.)**

4. When applying makeup, the ideal lighting conditions are the same as or close to those of (A) *your customary dressing room* (B) *the actual production environment* (C) *normal 3,200K studio lights.*

5. When working with a small single-chip camcorder under low-light conditions, you should avoid wearing saturated (A) *red* (B) *green* (C) *blue.*

6. You can counteract a heavy five-o'clock shadow by applying a light layer of (A) *yellow* (B) *skin-colored* (C) *bluish* pan-stick.

7. Under high-color-temperature lighting, use (A) *cool* (B) *warm* (C) *neutral* makeup colors.

8. As a weathercaster you can wear green so long as the chroma-key backdrop is (A) *blue* (B) *green* (C) *evenly lighted.*

1 ◯ ◯ ◯
   A   B   C

2 ◯ ◯
   A   B
◯ ◯ ◯ ◯
C D E F

3 ◯ ◯
   A   B
◯ ◯ ◯ ◯
C D E F

4 ◯ ◯ ◯
   A   B   C

5 ◯ ◯ ◯
   A   B   C

6 ◯ ◯ ◯
   A   B   C

7 ◯ ◯ ◯
   A   B   C

8 ◯ ◯ ◯
   A   B   C

SECTION TOTAL [ ]

REVIEW QUIZ

*Mark the following statements as true or false by filling in the bubbles in the **T** (for true) or*
***F** (for false) column.*

		T	F
1.	Talent includes both performers and actors.	1 ○	○
2.	When on a close-up, you must pick up the item you are demonstrating and hold it close to the camera lens.	2 ○	○
3.	To maintain sound perspective, you should talk louder when the camera is farther away from you and more softly when the camera is close to you.	3 ○	○
4.	When you work with a teleprompter, it is best to move the camera as close to the talent as possible.	4 ○	○
5.	When asked to give an audio level, you should count quickly to 10.	5 ○	○
6.	In an unrehearsed show, you can give the crew and the director a verbal warning cue of what you are going to do next.	6 ○	○
7.	When the camera is relatively far from you, you should walk toward it for good close-ups.	7 ○	○
8.	When you are on the air in a dramatic role, you must follow the rehearsed blocking precisely.	8 ○	○
9.	When demonstrating a small object, you can help the director by asking that the camera move a little closer.	9 ○	○
10.	Television actors always portray someone else.	10 ○	○
11.	What you wear when auditioning for a role is unimportant.	11 ○	○
12.	When on a panel, you should reposition the desk mic so that it points directly at you.	12 ○	○

SECTION TOTAL [   ]

PROBLEM-SOLVING APPLICATIONS

1. To practice blocking, write down a series of moves that carry you around your kitchen. For example, you can start at the stove, then get the teakettle out of the cupboard, fill it with water, and put it on the stove, go back to pick up the telephone, put down the telephone to answer the door, and so forth. Try to hit the same marks each time you go through the routine. If possible, have a friend video-record your blocking maneuvers from the same camera position. You can then compare the recordings and check how accurate your blocking was. As part of the same exercise, you can use various props (kitchen utensils) to see how the camera's field of view (LS to ECU) will influence your handling of them.

2. Use a product of your choice and video-record your pitch. What do you like about your performance? What don't you like? How could you improve your performance?

3. Pretend that you, person A, are receiving a telephone call from person B. In this scene we see and hear only person A (you). Using exactly the same dialogue (see the script on the following page), adapt your delivery and acting style to at least two of the following circumstances:

   a. B calls to tell you that he/she has just got an exciting new job.

   b. B calls to tell you that he/she has just lost his/her job.

   c. B has just had an accident with your new car.

   d. B has broken the engagement.

   e. B has won first prize in a video competition.

   Locate the scene anywhere you like. You may do well to write the other part of the phone conversation so that you can "listen" to the virtual B part of the dialogue and respond more convincingly verbally and nonverbally.

4. Have a friend take close-ups of you when you do the phone exercise and compare your expressions when the phone call brings happy news and unhappy news.

5. An experienced stage director, who is directing an adaptation of a stage play for TV, tells the lead actress that her facial expressions are not big enough to "reach the last row." What is your reaction? Be specific.

```
PHONE CONVERSATION
PERSON A
Hello?
Hi.
Fine, and you?
Good.
No.
No, really. It's always good to hear from you.
I beg your pardon?
You must be kidding.
Yes.
No.
What does Alex say to all this?
No. Should I?
I don't know.
Perhaps.
You want me to come over now?
Yes. Really.
Well, this changes things somewhat.
I think so.
I'm not so sure.
Yes. No. I...
All right. But not...
OK.
If you think this is...
Definitely.
Good-bye...When?
No. Really.
Good-bye.
```

Course No. _____ Date _____ Name _____

16 The Director in Production

REVIEW OF KEY TERMS

Match each term with its appropriate definition by filling in the corresponding bubble.

(A) walk-through   (D) dress rehearsal   (G) running time
(B) intercom   (E) single-camera directing   (H) schedule time
(C) camera rehearsal   (F) dry run   (I) multicamera directing

1. a full rehearsal with cameras and other pieces of production equipment

     1   ◯ ◯ ◯ ◯ ◯   A B C D E   ◯ ◯ ◯ ◯   F G H I

2. a rehearsal without equipment

     2   ◯ ◯ ◯ ◯ ◯   A B C D E   ◯ ◯ ◯ ◯   F G H I

3. full rehearsal with talent made-up and dressed

     3   ◯ ◯ ◯ ◯ ◯   A B C D E   ◯ ◯ ◯ ◯   F G H I

4. a system widely used by all production and technical personnel so that they can communicate with one another during a show

     4   ◯ ◯ ◯ ◯ ◯   A B C D E   ◯ ◯ ◯ ◯   F G H I

PAGE TOTAL [ ]

© 2015 Cengage Learning

(A) walk-through	(D) dress rehearsal	(G) running time
(B) intercom	(E) single-camera directing	(H) schedule time
(C) camera rehearsal	(F) dry run	(I) multicamera directing

5. an orientation session on the set with the production crew and talent

5 Ⓐ Ⓑ Ⓒ Ⓓ Ⓔ
  A B C D E
  Ⓕ Ⓖ Ⓗ Ⓘ
  F G H I

6. the times when a program starts and stops

6 Ⓐ Ⓑ Ⓒ Ⓓ Ⓔ
  A B C D E
  Ⓕ Ⓖ Ⓗ Ⓘ
  F G H I

7. the coordination of one camera for takes that are separately recorded for postproduction

7 Ⓐ Ⓑ Ⓒ Ⓓ Ⓔ
  A B C D E
  Ⓕ Ⓖ Ⓗ Ⓘ
  F G H I

8. duration of a program or program segment

8 Ⓐ Ⓑ Ⓒ Ⓓ Ⓔ
  A B C D E
  Ⓕ Ⓖ Ⓗ Ⓘ
  F G H I

9. the simultaneous coordination of two or more cameras for instantaneous editing

9 Ⓐ Ⓑ Ⓒ Ⓓ Ⓔ
  A B C D E
  Ⓕ Ⓖ Ⓗ Ⓘ
  F G H I

PAGE TOTAL

SECTION TOTAL

REVIEW OF DIRECTOR'S TERMINOLOGY

1. **Director's visualization cues.** From the list below, select the cue necessary to adjust the picture on the left screen to the picture on the right screen (in pairs from **a** through **l**) and fill in the bubbles with the corresponding letters.

(A) pedestal down
    or crane down
(B) tilt down
(C) tilt up
(D) zoom out

(E) truck right
(F) pedestal up
    or crane up
(G) dolly in
(H) pan left

(I) dolly out
(J) arc left
(K) pan right
(L) zoom in

a.

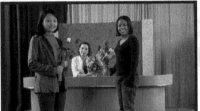 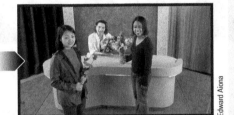

Edward Aiona

1a
○ ○ ○ ○
A B C D
○ ○ ○ ○
E F G H
○ ○ ○ ○
I J K L

b.

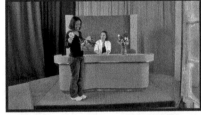 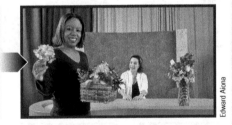

Edward Aiona

1b
○ ○ ○ ○
A B C D
○ ○ ○ ○
E F G H
○ ○ ○ ○
I J K L

c.

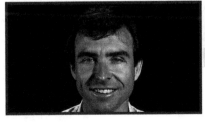 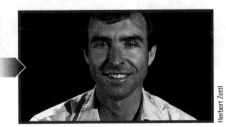

Herbert Zettl

1c
○ ○ ○ ○
A B C D
○ ○ ○ ○
E F G H
○ ○ ○ ○
I J K L

PAGE
TOTAL [   ]

(A) pedestal down
　　 or crane down
(B) tilt down
(C) tilt up
(D) zoom out

(E) truck right
(F) pedestal up
　　 or crane up
(G) dolly in
(H) pan left

(I) dolly out
(J) arc left
(K) pan right
(L) zoom in

d.

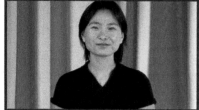 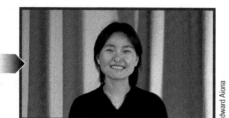

Edward Aiona

1d
A ○ B ○ C ○ D ○
E ○ F ○ G ○ H ○
I ○ J ○ K ○ L ○

e.

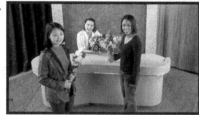 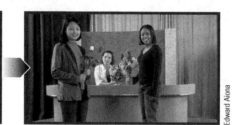

Edward Aiona

1e
A ○ B ○ C ○ D ○
E ○ F ○ G ○ H ○
I ○ J ○ K ○ L ○

f.

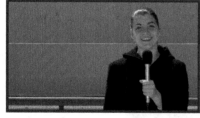 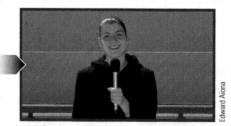

Edward Aiona

1f
A ○ B ○ C ○ D ○
E ○ F ○ G ○ H ○
I ○ J ○ K ○ L ○

PAGE TOTAL ▢

g.

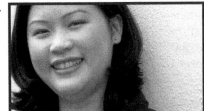
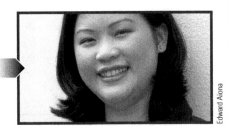

Edward Aiona

1g
- A ○ B ○ C ○ D ○
- E ○ F ○ G ○ H ○
- I ○ J ○ K ○ L ○

h.

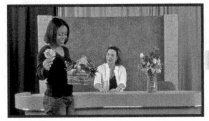
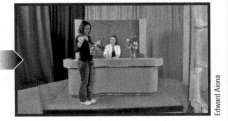

Edward Aiona

1h
- A ○ B ○ C ○ D ○
- E ○ F ○ G ○ H ○
- I ○ J ○ K ○ L ○

i.

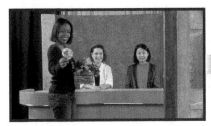
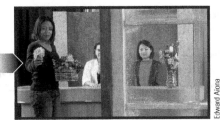

Edward Aiona

1i
- A ○ B ○ C ○ D ○
- E ○ F ○ G ○ H ○
- I ○ J ○ K ○ L ○

j.

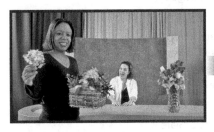
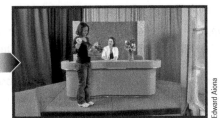

Edward Aiona

1j
- A ○ B ○ C ○ D ○
- E ○ F ○ G ○ H ○
- I ○ J ○ K ○ L ○

k.

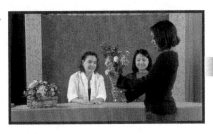
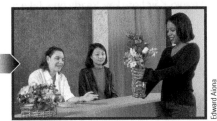

Edward Aiona

1k
- A ○ B ○ C ○ D ○
- E ○ F ○ G ○ H ○
- I ○ J ○ K ○ L ○

PAGE
TOTAL

(A)	pedestal down or crane down	(E)	truck right	(I)	dolly out
(B)	tilt down	(F)	pedestal up or crane up	(J)	arc left
(C)	tilt up	(G)	dolly in	(K)	pan right
(D)	zoom out	(H)	pan left	(L)	zoom in

 1.

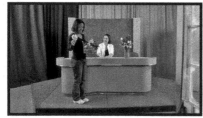 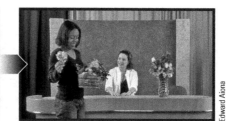

Edward Aiona

1l ○ A ○ B ○ C ○ D
○ E ○ F ○ G ○ H
○ I ○ J ○ K ○ L

2. Director's sequencing cues.

a. From the list below, select the director who uses the correct sequence of cues for the opening of a two-camera (C1 and C2) interview and fill in the corresponding bubble. *(There is a title key for the guest. Assume that the crew has received a general standby cue and that bars and tone have already been recorded by the AD.)*

(A) *Director A:* "Ready to take CG. Slate. Take slate. Ready black. Black. Beeper. Ready to come up on one CU of host—take one. Cue host. Ready two [on guest]. Take two. Cue guest. Key title. Take one."

(B) *Director B:* "Ready VR. Roll VR. Ready slate CG. Take slate—read slate. Ready black, ready beeper. [During the countdown] Ready one on Bill [host]. [During last two seconds of countdown] Cue Bill, up on one. Ready key [Bill]. Key. Lose key—change page. Ready two on Lynn, ready key CG [Lynn]. Take two—key—lose key. Ready one. Take one. Two, two-shot. Ready two, Take two."

(C) *Director C:* "Ready to roll video recorder. Roll video recorder. Ready CG. Slate. Read slate. Ready black. Ready beeper. To black. Beeper. Ready to come up on one. Up on one. Ready two. Take two. Key. Lose key. Ready one. Take one."

2a ○ A   ○ B   ○ C

b. From the list below, select the correct director's cues for transitions by filling in the corresponding bubbles. *(Multiple answers are possible.)*

2b ○ ○ ○ ○ ○
    A B C D E

(A) "Ready to take camera two. Take camera two."

(B) "Ready three. Take three."

(C) "Ready diamond wipe. Dissolve wipe."

(D) "Ready to go to black. Go to black."

(E) "Ready wipe. Dissolve to two."

c. From the list below, select the correct director's cues to the floor manager by filling in the corresponding bubbles. The talent are Mary, Lisa, John, and Larry. *(Multiple answers are possible.)*

2c ○ ○ ○ ○ ○
    A B C D E

(A) "Ready to cue Mary. Cue Mary."

(B) "Ready to cue him. Cue him."

(C) "Make him talk faster."

(D) "Move her stage-right."

(E) "Give Lisa the wind-up."

3. Director's cues to floor manager concerning the positioning of props. Select the appropriate cue to the floor manager to adjust the position of the prop shown on the left screen to that of the right screen and fill in the bubbles with the corresponding letters.

(A) "Turn the sculpture counterclockwise."
(B) "Turn the sculpture clockwise."

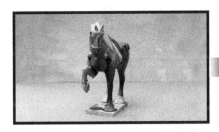 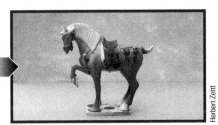

Herbert Zettl

3 ○   ○
  A   B

P A G E
T O T A L [   ]

4. **Director's cues to the floor manager concerning the positioning of talent.** From the list below, select the appropriate cue to the floor manager to adjust the position of the talent shown on the left screen to that of the right screen (in pairs **a** through **c**) and fill in the bubbles with the corresponding letters.

(A) "Have talent turn in [toward the camera]."
(B) "Have talent move left."

a.

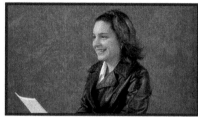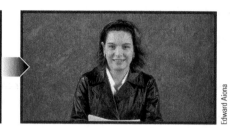

Edward Aiona

4a ◯ ◯
    A   B

(A) "Have woman turn to her left."
(B) "Have camera arc right."

b.

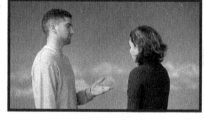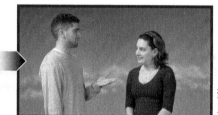

Edward Aiona

4b ◯ ◯
    A   B

(A) "Pan right."
(B) "Move talent to camera right."

c.

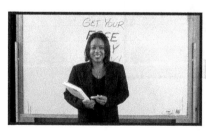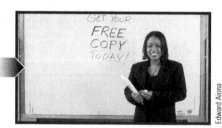

Edward Aiona

4c ◯ ◯
    A   B

PAGE
TOTAL

SECTION
TOTAL

REVIEW OF REHEARSAL TECHNIQUES

Select the correct answers and fill in the bubbles with the corresponding letters.

1. Rehearsals that combine walk-throughs and camera rehearsal are most efficiently conducted from the (A) *studio floor* (B) *rehearsal hall* (C) *control room.*

   1 ○ A ○ B ○ C

2. When breaking down an EFP script for a single-camera production, you should
   (A) *start with the most interesting parts to take advantage of the talent's creative energy*
   (B) *combine all scenes that play at the same location and/or with the same talent*
   (C) *try to maintain the narrative order of the scenes.*

   2 ○ A ○ B ○ C

3. When doing a single-camera ENG or EFP, you should (A) *always get a fair amount of cutaways* (B) *get cutaways only if you think your shots will not cut together well* (C) *not bother with cutaways if you have plenty of time for postproduction.*

   3 ○ A ○ B ○ C

4. When scheduling "notes" segments in your time line, you need to also schedule
   (A) *additional talent rehearsal time* (B) *additional technical rehearsal time* (C) *reset time.*

   4 ○ A ○ B ○ C

5. When engaged in a standard EFP, you need not worry about (A) *talent and technical walk-throughs* (B) *cross-overs from one location to the next* (C) *an extensive intercom setup.*

   5 ○ A ○ B ○ C

6. Camera rehearsal is conducted (A) *for all technical operations but without talent* (B) *for cameras only* (C) *similar to a dress rehearsal.*

   6 ○ A ○ B ○ C

7. Blocking rehearsals are most efficiently conducted (A) *from the control room* (B) *on the actual studio set* (C) *on the studio floor or in the rehearsal hall.*

   7 ○ A ○ B ○ C

8. When calling for a "take," you should pause between the "ready" and the "take" cues (A) *as little as possible* (B) *until you see the TD put his finger on the correct switcher button* (C) *for at least five seconds.*

   8 ○ A ○ B ○ C

9. When doing a walk-through/camera rehearsal combination from the studio floor, you should give (A) *all cues as though you were directing from the control room* (B) *only the talent cues* (C) *only the camera cues.*

   9 ○ A ○ B ○ C

10. If pressed for time, you should call for (A) *an uninterrupted camera rehearsal* (B) *a walk-through/camera rehearsal combination* (C) *a blocking rehearsal.*

    10 ○ A ○ B ○ C

SECTION TOTAL [ ]

1. Assume that the following six shots represent a sequence of video inputs on the preview monitor in the order you will switch them to the line-out. Using the floor plan below, specify the cameras and the other video inputs used for the shots. Note that one video input does not originate in the studio and another uses two video sources simultaneously. *(Multiple answers are possible.)*

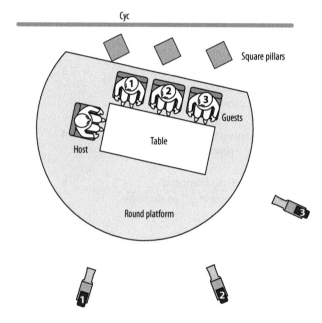

Sources: (A) camera 1

(B) camera 2

(C) camera 3

(D) video recording 1

(E) CG

a.

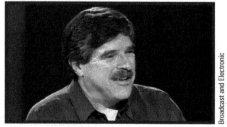

Host

Broadcast and Electronic Communication Arts Department at San Francisco State University

1a ○ ○ ○ ○ ○
    A B C D E

P A G E
T O T A L

b.   Guest 1

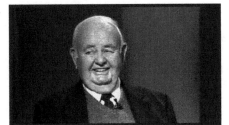

1b ○ ○ ○ ○ ○
    A B C D E

c.

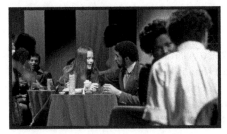

1c ○ ○ ○ ○ ○
    A B C D E

d.   Guest 2

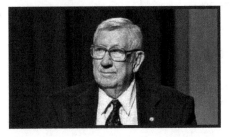

1d ○ ○ ○ ○ ○
    A B C D E

e.

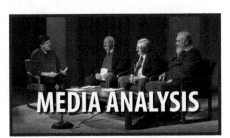

MEDIA ANALYSIS

1e ○ ○ ○ ○ ○
    A B C D E

f.   Guest 3

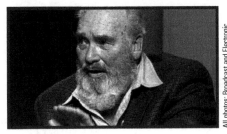

All photos: Broadcast and Electronic Communication Arts Department at San Francisco State University

1f ○ ○ ○ ○ ○
    A B C D E

| PAGE TOTAL | |
| SECTION TOTAL | |

Select the correct answers and fill in the bubbles with the corresponding letters.

1. In the noon newscast, you must switch to the first 3-minute satellite feed at exactly 3:45 minutes into the show and the second feed at 15:15 minutes after the end of the first one. You need to switch to the remote feeds at:

   (A) 12:03:45 and 12:19:00

   (B) 12:03:45 and 12:22:00

   (C) 12:03:45 and 12:15:15

   1 ○ ○ ○
       A B C

2. The log indicates that the *Women: Face-to-Face* program ends at 11:26:30. A large part of the program is taken up by a fashion show. The fashion coordinator would like a 1-minute, a 30-second, and a 15-second cue as well as a cut at the end of her segment. The regular program host, who follows the fashion show with a 1½-minute closing, would like a 30-second and a 15-second cue and a cut at the end of the program. From the list below, select the correct clock times for the cues.

   (A) 11:24:00, 11:24:30, 11:24:45, 11:25:00 and 11:26:00, 11:26:15, 11:26:30

   (B) 11:24:30, 11:25:00, 11:25:45, 11:26:00 and 11:26:15, 11:26:30

   (C) 11:22:00, 11:23:00, 11:24:00, 11:24:30 and 11:25:00, 11:26:00, 11:26:15

   2 ○ ○ ○
       A B C

3. *Subjective time* refers to (A) *the running time of the show segment* (B) *how fast or slowly the segment seems to move* (C) *how the parts of the segment relate to one another.*

   3 ○ ○ ○
       A B C

SECTION TOTAL [ ]

REVIEW OF SINGLE-CAMERA DIRECTING

Select the correct answers and fill in the bubbles with the corresponding letters.

1. When directing single-camera style, you (A) *need to be concerned about continuity of widely dispersed shots* (B) *can do away with cutaways* (C) *can visualize each shot independently of all others.*

2. When directing single-camera style in the field, you are aided most effectively by (A) *having the camera hooked up to a field monitor* (B) *using the camera viewfinder to correct shots* (C) *using only a director's viewfinder.*

3. When directing single-camera style, you should (A) *rehearse each shot before the take* (B) *rehearse all shots before ever activating the camera* (C) *rehearse the shots in the order of the storyboard narrative.*

4. In single-camera directing, you should slate (A) *each shot* (B) *each take* (C) *each scene.*

5. In single-camera directing, camera placement is (A) *not important because you are shooting from various angles anyway* (B) *very important to ensure continuity* (C) *determined primarily by where the actors are.*

6. When directing single-camera style in the studio, the most effective way is to rehearse and direct each shot (A) *always from the control room* (B) *always from the studio floor* (C) *from either the control room or the studio floor.*

7. When recording out of sequence, you will find (A) *a large external viewfinder* (B) *a storyboard* (C) *the PA's notes* especially helpful for your visualization.

	A	B	C
1	○	○	○
2	○	○	○
3	○	○	○
4	○	○	○
5	○	○	○
6	○	○	○
7	○	○	○

SECTION TOTAL [ ]

REVIEW QUIZ

*Mark the following statements as true or false by filling in the bubbles in the **T** (for true) or **F** (for false) column.*

	T	F
1. During a walk-through/camera rehearsal combination, the director rehearses primarily from the studio floor.	○	○
2. To save time in a studio rehearsal, you should use the SA system as often as possible.	○	○
3. When directing from the control room, you should address the name of the camera operator rather than the camera number to get efficient camera action.	○	○
4. When directing a studio show, the SA system is more appropriate than the PL system.	○	○
5. When directing a daily newscast, you do not need a floor plan to preplan the camera shots.	○	○
6. Even with an efficient intercom system, the switcher should always be located right next to the director's position.	○	○
7. When directing a fully scripted show, you should pay more attention to the script than the preview or line monitors.	○	○
8. The floor manager's cues are especially important when engaged in single-camera EFP.	○	○
9. Even when doing an EFP, you should check the video recording to see whether the preceding scene was properly recorded before moving to the next location.	○	○
10. Keeping accurate running time is more important in directing a live multicamera show than a single-camera EFP.	○	○
11. Cutaways are especially important in film-style shooting.	○	○
12. When doing an EFP, the talent and technical walk-throughs are less important than when doing a studio show.	○	○
13. When directing a single-camera EFP, a properly working intercom system is one of the most essential setup items.	○	○
14. An external monitor that carries the camera's video greatly facilitates single-camera directing.	○	○
15. You should tell the floor manager whenever there is a technical problem that you need to solve from the control room.	○	○

SECTION TOTAL [ ]

PROBLEM-SOLVING APPLICATIONS

1. Mark a scene from a fully scripted TV play and practice calling the shots.

2. During the video-recording of the first scene of a demanding outdoor EFP for a car commercial, the audio person suggests doing a retake because she picked up a brief, distant jet sound. Would you recommend a retake? If so, why? If not, why not?

3. During the evening news, the wrong video-recorded story comes up. What can you do?

4. During an O/S sequence in a multicamera dramatic production, one of the actors has trouble hitting the blocking marks and is frequently obscured by the camera-near person. What advice would you give the actor?

5. Get a published script of an episode of a drama or soap opera and mark it for three-camera and single-camera directing.

6. The director uses one set of commands during rehearsal but switches to another when doing the on-the-air show. Which potential problems do you foresee, if any? Be specific.

7. The producer suggests that you should not waste valuable time by doing a walk-through/camera rehearsal from the studio floor but skip right to the camera rehearsal from the control room. What is your reaction? Why?

8. When checking all the intercom systems before a remote live multicamera telecast of a large political gathering at city hall, the talent's IFB interrupts itself from time to time. What backup cueing device would you recommend that close to airtime?

9. When pressed for time, the director decides to conduct the rehearsal from the studio floor. Would you agree or disagree with such a move? Be specific. How, if at all, would the director's request affect the studio equipment and the control room activities?

10. The floor manager expresses her concern to you, the director, about the lack of adequate intercom facilities for an EFP of the local garden show. How would you respond?

11. The line producer of a complex commercial considers the director's explaining the process message to talent and crew a waste of time. What is your reaction? Be specific.

17 Field Production and Big Remotes

REVIEW OF KEY TERMS

Match each term with its appropriate definition by filling in the corresponding bubble.

(A) broadband
(B) DBS
(C) downlink
(D) microwave relay
(E) remote survey

(F) iso camera
(G) mini-link
(H) field production
(I) big remote
(J) instant replay

(K) Ku-band
(L) uplink
(M) live recording
(N) location sketch
(O) VJ

1. a preproduction on-location investigation of the existing facilities of a scheduled telecast

1
A ○ B ○ C ○ D ○ E ○
F ○ G ○ H ○ I ○ J ○
K ○ L ○ M ○ N ○ O ○

2. the continuous recording of a live TV pickup for later playback

2
A ○ B ○ C ○ D ○ E ○
F ○ G ○ H ○ I ○ J ○
K ○ L ○ M ○ N ○ O ○

3. a hand-drawn map of the remote locale

3
A ○ B ○ C ○ D ○ E ○
F ○ G ○ H ○ I ○ J ○
K ○ L ○ M ○ N ○ O ○

PAGE TOTAL ☐

(A) broadband	(F) iso camera	(K) Ku-band
(B) DBS	(G) mini-link	(L) uplink
(C) downlink	(H) field production	(M) live recording
(D) microwave relay	(I) big remote	(N) location sketch
(E) remote survey	(J) instant replay	(O) VJ

4. an antenna and equipment that receives the signals coming from a satellite

4
A B C D E
F G H I J
K L M N O

5. often used in sports remotes; feeds into the switcher and its own video recorder

5
A B C D E
F G H I J
K L M N O

6. a setup of several small microwave transmitters and receivers to transport the television signal around obstacles

6
A B C D E
F G H I J
K L M N O

7. a news reporter who shoots, edits, and writes his or her own video packages

7
A B C D E
F G H I J
K L M N O

8. a variety of information sent simultaneously over a fiber-optic cable

8
A B C D E
F G H I J
K L M N O

PAGE TOTAL

206

CHAPTER 17   FIELD PRODUCTION AND BIG REMOTES

9. an earth station transmitter used to send video and audio signals to a satellite

9 A ○ B ○ C ○ D ○ E ○
F ○ G ○ H ○ I ○ J ○
K ○ L ○ M ○ N ○ O ○

10. a high-frequency signal used by satellites

10 A ○ B ○ C ○ D ○ E ○
F ○ G ○ H ○ I ○ J ○
K ○ L ○ M ○ N ○ O ○

11. a production outside the studio to televise live and/or live-record a large scheduled event

11 A ○ B ○ C ○ D ○ E ○
F ○ G ○ H ○ I ○ J ○
K ○ L ○ M ○ N ○ O ○

12. a satellite with a high-powered transponder

12 A ○ B ○ C ○ D ○ E ○
F ○ G ○ H ○ I ○ J ○
K ○ L ○ M ○ N ○ O ○

13. any production that occurs outside the studio

13 A ○ B ○ C ○ D ○ E ○
F ○ G ○ H ○ I ○ J ○
K ○ L ○ M ○ N ○ O ○

14. repeating a key play or an important event for the viewer by playing it back immediately after its live occurrence

14 A ○ B ○ C ○ D ○ E ○
F ○ G ○ H ○ I ○ J ○
K ○ L ○ M ○ N ○ O ○

PAGE TOTAL [   ]

(A) broadband   (F) iso camera   (K) Ku-band
(B) DBS   (G) mini-link   (L) uplink
(C) downlink   (H) field production   (M) live recording
(D) microwave relay   (I) big remote   (N) location sketch
(E) remote survey   (J) instant replay   (O) VJ

15. a signal transport from the remote location to the station or transmitter in various transmission steps

15
○ ○ ○ ○ ○
A   B   C   D   E
○ ○ ○ ○ ○
F   G   H   I   J
○ ○ ○ ○ ○
K   L   M   N   O

PAGE TOTAL

SECTION TOTAL

REVIEW OF FIELD PRODUCTION

Select the correct answers and fill in the bubbles with the corresponding letters.

1. Instant replays are most common in (A) *big remotes* (B) *EFP* (C) *ENG.*

2. The field production that almost always requires careful postproduction is (A) *ENG* (B) *big remotes* (C) *EFP.*

3. The field production that affords the most control over the event is (A) *ENG* (B) *EFP* (C) *big remotes.*

4. The walk-through rehearsal is least important for (A) *ENG* (B) *EFP* (C) *big remotes.*

5. The remote system least likely to use signal transmission equipment is (A) *ENG* (B) *EFP* (C) *big remotes.*

6. The directing procedure that most closely resembles multicamera studio production is (A) *ENG* (B) *EFP* (C) *big remotes.*

7. The most flexible type of field production that needs little or no preproduction is (A) *ENG* (B) *EFP* (C) *big remotes.*

8. A floor manager is most important in (A) *ENG* (B) *EFP* (C) *big remotes.*

9. The normal transmission equipment in ENG vans is (A) *a microwave transmitter* (B) *a satellite uplink* (C) *fiber-optic cable.*

10. Because the camera setup is done by technical personnel, the director is (A) *not needed* (B) *very important* (C) *consulted only in emergencies* when choosing the specific locations for the key cameras.

11. A remote survey requires (A) *only a production survey* (B) *only a technical survey* (C) *both a production and a technical survey.*

12. A complex intercommunication system is most important for (A) *ENG* (B) *EFP* (C) *big remotes.*

13. To ensure access to the event location, you need (A) *a contact person* (B) *a written statement from the producer* (C) *an OK from the chief of police.*

14. When using multiple cameras or camcorders in EFP, the cameras (A) *shoot a scene simultaneously* (B) *must feed a switcher* (C) *run in sync.*

#	A	B	C
1	○	○	○
2	○	○	○
3	○	○	○
4	○	○	○
5	○	○	○
6	○	○	○
7	○	○	○
8	○	○	○
9	○	○	○
10	○	○	○
11	○	○	○
12	○	○	○
13	○	○	○
14	○	○	○

SECTION TOTAL [   ]

1. Analyze the following six location sketches for field productions and big remotes. Evaluate the type and the position of each camera by the criteria listed below and fill in the bubbles with the corresponding letters. *(Multiple answers are possible.)*

   (A) camera position OK
   (B) wrong or unnecessary camera position
   (C) inappropriate camera type
   (D) cable hazard
   (E) lighting problems (shooting into the sun or against another strong light source)

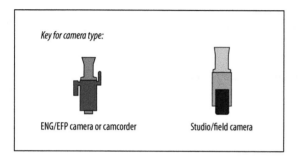

Key for camera type:

ENG/EFP camera or camcorder   Studio/field camera

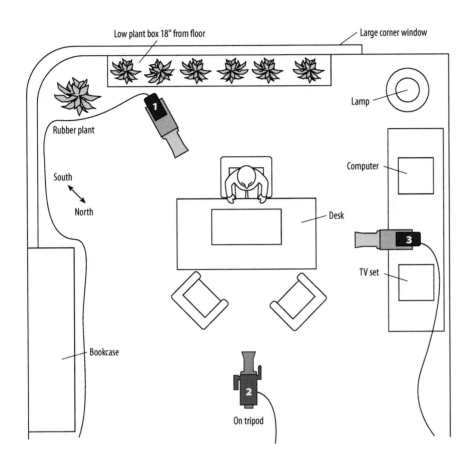

Low plant box 18" from floor

Large corner window

Rubber plant

South ↕ North

Lamp

Computer

Desk

TV set

Bookcase

On tripod

EFP of Company President's Address to Employees
Live-recorded for minimal postproduction
Recording date: July 15
Recording time: 2:30 p.m. to 4:30 p.m.
Place: President's office, Tower Building, 34th floor

a. comments on C1

b. comments on C2

c. comments on C3

1a **C1** ○ ○ ○
           A B C
         ○ ○
         D E

1b **C2** ○ ○ ○
           A B C
         ○ ○
         D E

1c **C3** ○ ○ ○
           A B C
         ○ ○
         D E

P A G E
T O T A L [   ]

© 2015 Cengage Learning

(A) camera position OK
(B) wrong or unnecessary camera position
(C) inappropriate camera type
(D) cable hazard
(E) lighting problems (shooting into the sun or against another strong light source)

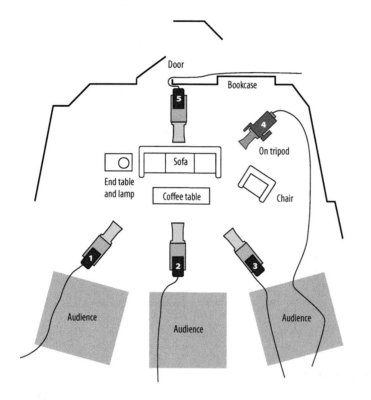

Play

Video-recording of two performances of a high-school play (situation comedy) with a live audience, minimal postproduction, and the use of a large remote truck

d. comments on C1

e. comments on C2

f. comments on C3

g. comments on C4

h. comments on C5

1d C1   ○ ○ ○
          A B C
          ○ ○
          D E

1e C2   ○ ○ ○
          A B C
          ○ ○
          D E

1f C3   ○ ○ ○
          A B C
          ○ ○
          D E

1g C4   ○ ○ ○
          A B C
          ○ ○
          D E

1h C5   ○ ○ ○
          A B C
          ○ ○
          D E

P A G E
T O T A L   [   ]

© 2015 Cengage Learning

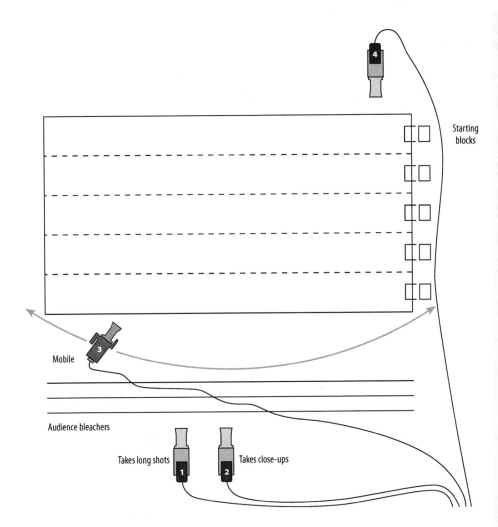

Starting blocks

Mobile

Audience bleachers

Takes long shots   Takes close-ups

Swim Meet
Live telecast of state swim meet; large indoor pool

    i. comments on C1

    j. comments on C2

    k. comments on C3

    l. comments on C4

1i C1 ○ ○ ○
      A B C
      ○ ○
      D E

1j C2 ○ ○ ○
      A B C
      ○ ○
      D E

1k C3 ○ ○ ○
      A B C
      ○ ○
      D E

1l C4 ○ ○ ○
      A B C
      ○ ○
      D E

PAGE TOTAL [   ]

(A) camera position OK
(B) wrong or unnecessary camera position
(C) inappropriate camera type
(D) cable hazard
(E) lighting problems (shooting into the sun or against another strong light source)

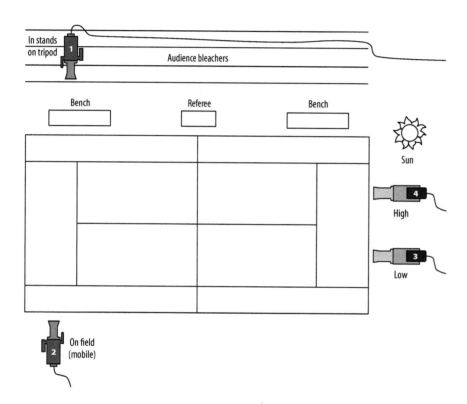

Tennis Match
Live coverage of tennis match

m. comments on C1

n. comments on C2

o. comments on C3

p. comments on C4

1m C1 ○ ○ ○
   A B C
   ○ ○
   D E

1n C2 ○ ○ ○
   A B C
   ○ ○
   D E

1o C3 ○ ○ ○
   A B C
   ○ ○
   D E

1p C4 ○ ○ ○
   A B C
   ○ ○
   D E

P A G E
T O T A L

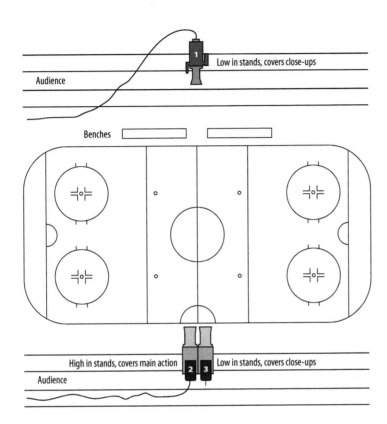

Low in stands, covers close-ups

Audience

Benches

High in stands, covers main action   Low in stands, covers close-ups

Audience

Ice-Hockey Game

Big remote live-recorded for broadcast with 10-second delay
Spectator stands on both sides of rink

q. comments on C1

r. comments on C2

s. comments on C3

1q C1 ○ ○ ○
        A B C
        ○ ○
        D E

1r C2 ○ ○ ○
        A B C
        ○ ○
        D E

1s C3 ○ ○ ○
        A B C
        ○ ○
        D E

PAGE
TOTAL [   ]

(A) camera position OK
(B) wrong or unnecessary camera position
(C) inappropriate camera type
(D) cable hazard
(E) lighting problems (shooting into the sun or against another strong light source)

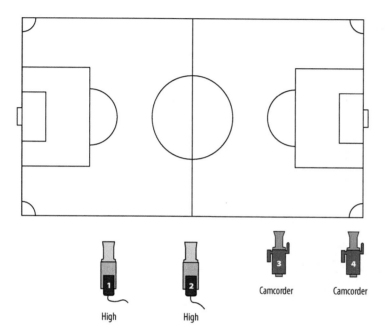

High   High   Camcorder   Camcorder

Soccer Practice

EFP of soccer practice for a show that demonstrates the beauty and the grace of a soccer game; heavy postproduction with effects and sound track

t. comments on C1

u. comments on C2

v. comments on C3

w. comments on C4

1t **C1** ◯ ◯ ◯
             A B C
           ◯ ◯
           D E

1u **C2** ◯ ◯ ◯
             A B C
           ◯ ◯
           D E

1v **C3** ◯ ◯ ◯
             A B C
           ◯ ◯
           D E

1w **C4** ◯ ◯ ◯
             A B C
           ◯ ◯
           D E

PAGE TOTAL

SECTION TOTAL

REVIEW OF FACILITIES REQUESTS

*Evaluate the equipment facilities requests for the three EFPs described below. Identify the **wrong** equipment and the items **not** needed and fill in the bubbles with the corresponding letters. **Multiple answers are possible.***

1. Midmorning recording of a brief dance number in front of city hall for a music video using ENG/EFP cameras, *not* camcorders

   Facilities Request 1
   (A) 3 video recorders
   (B) 6 shotgun mics
   (C) jib arm
   (D) 3 ENG/EFP cameras
   (E) 3 RCUs, connecting cables, and portable monitors
   (F) large audio mixer
   (G) portable lighting kit
   (H) PA audio playback system
   (I) CG

   1 ○ ○ ○ ○ ○
      A B C D E
      ○ ○ ○ ○
      F G H I

2. Taped interview of a media scholar in his hotel room for news item

   Facilities Request 2
   (A) camcorder
   (B) iso video recorder
   (C) portable lighting kit
   (D) RCU
   (E) 2 lavalier mics
   (F) portable audio mixer
   (G) recording media
   (H) batteries
   (I) preview monitors

   2 ○ ○ ○ ○ ○
      A B C D E
      ○ ○ ○ ○
      F G H I

3. Live stand-up traffic report from downtown during the afternoon rush hour

   Facilities Request 3
   (A) camcorder
   (B) 2 video recorders
   (C) shotgun mic (camera mic)
   (D) hand mic
   (E) 3 portable lighting kits
   (F) audiotape recorder
   (G) microwave transmission equipment
   (H) IFB intercom
   (I) CG

   3 ○ ○ ○ ○ ○
      A B C D E
      ○ ○ ○ ○
      F G H I

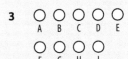

SECTION
TOTAL

REVIEW OF SIGNAL TRANSPORT SYSTEMS

Select the correct answers and fill in the bubbles with the corresponding letters.

1. The Ku-band operates on a frequency that is (A) *higher than* (B) *lower than* (C) *the same as* the frequency for the C-band and is (D) *more stable in bad weather* (E) *less stable in bad weather* (F) *immune to weather conditions.* **(Fill in two bubbles.)**

2. The C-band uplink and downlink dishes are (A) *the same as* (B) *smaller than* (C) *larger than* the ones for the Ku-band.

3. Small uplink trucks use (A) *the Ku-band* (B) *the C-band* (C) *their own satellite frequency* for signal transmission.

4. EFP makes (A) *more frequent use of satellite transmission than* (B) *less frequent use of satellite transmission than* (C) *about the same amount of satellite transmission as* big remotes.

5. A microwave signal (A) *can* (B) *cannot* be blocked by big buildings or mountains.

6. A mini-link refers to (A) *a small uplink* (B) *a small downlink* (C) *several microwave links to transport the signal around an obstacle.*

7. When stringing cables is prohibited, an EFP camera can use (A) *its own small transmitter* (B) *a C-band uplink* (C) *a Ku-band satellite* to transmit its signal over short distances.

1 ○ A	○ B	○ C
○ D	○ E	○ F
2 ○ A	○ B	○ C
3 ○ A	○ B	○ C
4 ○ A	○ B	○ C
5 ○ A	○ B	
6 ○ A	○ B	○ C
7 ○ A	○ B	○ C

SECTION TOTAL [　　　]

REVIEW QUIZ

*Mark the following statements as true or false by filling in the bubbles in the **T** (for true) or*
***F** (for false) column.*

		T	F
1.	Big remote trucks usually contain an audio control, a video-recording control, a program control, and a technical control with signal transmission equipment.	○	○
2.	Remote surveys are relatively unimportant for EFP.	○	○
3.	Iso cameras cannot be used for the regular coverage of a remote telecast.	○	○
4.	So long as you have good headsets, you do not need other intercom systems on big remotes.	○	○
5.	When shooting a single-camera EFP for postproduction, you do not need extensive intercom systems.	○	○
6.	So long as you use an IFB system, the floor manager is unnecessary for big remotes.	○	○
7.	The contact person is important only in preproduction.	○	○
8.	If possible, you should do the survey for an outdoor remote during the time the actual production will take place.	○	○
9.	The CG operator is especially important during a live broadcast of a football game.	○	○
10.	Remote surveys are relatively unimportant for ENG.	○	○
11.	To make the remote telecast as exciting as possible, you should use as many cameras as are available.	○	○
12.	You need a switcher when using three EFP cameras as multiple isos.	○	○
13.	So long as you have a good transmission system, you do not need video recorders in the remote truck.	○	○
14.	A careful audio setup is as important as the camera setup in big remotes.	○	○

SECTION
TOTAL

PROBLEM-SOLVING APPLICATIONS

1. To get a good overhead shot of a parade, you, the director, would like to place one of the cameras on the balcony of a twentieth-floor window of a nearby hotel. The TD informs you that the hotel manager has nothing against your renting the room for the day and setting up the camera, but she will not allow any cable runs either inside or outside the hotel. What would you suggest?

2. The producer learns at the last minute that the president of the European Union will arrive at the international airport and wants you to cover her arrival live. According to the producer, you should have no problem with the transmission because the station's transmitter is in line-of-sight of the airport. What field production method would you recommend? Specifically, what equipment and personnel would you need to accomplish this assignment?

3. You are the director for the live multicamera coverage of a large computer convention. While you are giving instructions to the talent to wind up her interview with one of the computer experts, her IFB fails. How else can you communicate with her while she is on the air?

4. Conduct a detailed remote survey for the live coverage of one of the following: (1) a football game, (2) a track meet, (3) a basketball game, (4) a baseball game, (5) a concert of a symphony orchestra, (6) an outdoor rock concert, or (7) a modern dance performance in a city park. Be sure to include all major production items, such as camera placement, audio and lighting requirements, intercom and transmission systems, power source, and so forth.

5. Prepare location sketches and facilities requests for the remote or EFP selected in the previous question.

18 Postproduction Editing: How It Works

REVIEW OF KEY TERMS

Match each term with its appropriate definition by filling in the corresponding bubble.

(A) EDL
(B) slate
(C) time code
(D) raw footage
(E) NLE
(F) take

(G) shot
(H) edit master recording
(I) split edit
(J) off-line editing
(K) window dub
(L) ADR

(M) source media
(N) capture
(O) vector
(P) on-line editing
(Q) clip

1. consists of edit-in and edit-out points expressed in time code numbers

1 (A) (B) (C) (D) (E)
   (F) (G) (H) (I) (J)
   (K) (L) (M) (N) (O)
   (P) (Q)

2. source material that is recorded uncompressed

2 (A) (B) (C) (D) (E)
   (F) (G) (H) (I) (J)
   (K) (L) (M) (N) (O)
   (P) (Q)

PAGE TOTAL ☐

(A) EDL	(G) shot	(M) source media
(B) slate	(H) edit master recording	(N) capture
(C) time code	(I) split edit	(O) vector
(D) raw footage	(J) off-line editing	(P) on-line editing
(E) NLE	(K) window dub	(Q) clip
(F) take	(L) ADR	

3. the interval between two transitions

3 Ⓐ Ⓑ Ⓒ Ⓓ Ⓔ Ⓕ Ⓖ Ⓗ Ⓘ Ⓙ Ⓚ Ⓛ Ⓜ Ⓝ Ⓞ Ⓟ Ⓠ

4. a "bumped-down" copy of all source recordings with the time code keyed over each frame

4 Ⓐ Ⓑ Ⓒ Ⓓ Ⓔ Ⓕ Ⓖ Ⓗ Ⓘ Ⓙ Ⓚ Ⓛ Ⓜ Ⓝ Ⓞ Ⓟ Ⓠ

5. a perceivable force with a direction and a magnitude

5 Ⓐ Ⓑ Ⓒ Ⓓ Ⓔ Ⓕ Ⓖ Ⓗ Ⓘ Ⓙ Ⓚ Ⓛ Ⓜ Ⓝ Ⓞ Ⓟ Ⓠ

6. recapturing the assembled shots at a higher resolution or creating a high-quality edit master recording

6 Ⓐ Ⓑ Ⓒ Ⓓ Ⓔ Ⓕ Ⓖ Ⓗ Ⓘ Ⓙ Ⓚ Ⓛ Ⓜ Ⓝ Ⓞ Ⓟ Ⓠ

P A G E
T O T A L

7. process that produces the EDL or a low-resolution capture

7 ⃝ ⃝ ⃝ ⃝ ⃝
   A B C D E
   ⃝ ⃝ ⃝ ⃝ ⃝
   F G H I J
   ⃝ ⃝ ⃝ ⃝ ⃝
   K L M N O
   ⃝ ⃝
   P Q

8. transferring video and audio information to a computer hard drive

8 ⃝ ⃝ ⃝ ⃝ ⃝
   A B C D E
   ⃝ ⃝ ⃝ ⃝ ⃝
   F G H I J
   ⃝ ⃝ ⃝ ⃝ ⃝
   K L M N O
   ⃝ ⃝
   P Q

9. similar repeated shots taken during video-recording or filming

9 ⃝ ⃝ ⃝ ⃝ ⃝
   A B C D E
   ⃝ ⃝ ⃝ ⃝ ⃝
   F G H I J
   ⃝ ⃝ ⃝ ⃝ ⃝
   K L M N O
   ⃝ ⃝
   P Q

10. allows instant random access to and easy rearrangement of shots

10 ⃝ ⃝ ⃝ ⃝ ⃝
    A B C D E
    ⃝ ⃝ ⃝ ⃝ ⃝
    F G H I J
    ⃝ ⃝ ⃝ ⃝ ⃝
    K L M N O
    ⃝ ⃝
    P Q

11. a shot or brief sequence of shots captured on the hard drive

11 ⃝ ⃝ ⃝ ⃝ ⃝
    A B C D E
    ⃝ ⃝ ⃝ ⃝ ⃝
    F G H I J
    ⃝ ⃝ ⃝ ⃝ ⃝
    K L M N O
    ⃝ ⃝
    P Q

PAGE
TOTAL [   ]

(A) EDL	(G) shot	(M) source media
(B) slate	(H) edit master recording	(N) capture
(C) time code	(I) split edit	(O) vector
(D) raw footage	(J) off-line editing	(P) on-line editing
(E) NLE	(K) window dub	(Q) clip
(F) take	(L) ADR	

12. audio precedes the shot or bleeds into the next one

12 A B C D E F G H I J K L M N O P Q

13. the media that contains the final on-line edit

13 A B C D E F G H I J K L M N O P Q

14. the recording devices (hard disk, optical disc, or memory card) that hold the recorded material

14 A B C D E F G H I J K L M N O P Q

15. a device that provides essential production information recorded at the beginning of each take

15 A B C D E F G H I J K L M N O P Q

PAGE TOTAL

16. the synchronization of speech with the lip movements of the speaker in postproduction

16 ○ ○ ○ ○ ○
   A B C D E
   ○ ○ ○ ○ ○
   F G H I J
   ○ ○ ○ ○ ○
   K L M N O
   ○ ○
   P Q

17. gives each video frame a specific address

17 ○ ○ ○ ○ ○
   A B C D E
   ○ ○ ○ ○ ○
   F G H I J
   ○ ○ ○ ○ ○
   K L M N O
   ○ ○
   P Q

PAGE TOTAL [ ]

SECTION TOTAL [ ]

REVIEW OF NONLINEAR EDITING

Select the correct answers and fill in the bubbles with the corresponding letters.

1. The VR log helps (A) *organize the source material* (B) *eliminate unimportant cutaways* (C) *locate specific shots during the editing process.*

    1 ◯ A ◯ B ◯ C

2. When the audio precedes a shot or blends into another, it is commonly called (A) *a split edit* (B) *a complexity edit* (C) *a continuity edit.*

    2 ◯ A ◯ B ◯ C

3. When editing video to audio, you use (A) *video as the A-roll and audio as the B-roll* (B) *audio as the A-roll and video as the B-roll* (C) *no A and B rolls.*

    3 ◯ A ◯ B ◯ C

4. In nonlinear editing, the timeline refers to the (A) *length of the clip* (B) *production schedule* (C) *video and audio tracks with their clips.*

    4 ◯ A ◯ B ◯ C

5. When importing source footage into the NLE system for off-line editing, you need to determine the (A) *nature of the source material* (B) *codec* (C) *drop frame or non–drop frame designation.*

    5 ◯ A ◯ B ◯ C

6. The operational principle of nonlinear editing is (A) *copying images from a source to a record device* (B) *rearranging audio and video data files* (C) *transferring digital data from a VR to a hard drive.*

    6 ◯ A ◯ B ◯ C

7. The time code frames and seconds roll over at (A) *29 frames, 59 seconds* (B) *29 frames, 29 seconds* (C) *59 frames, 59 seconds.*

    7 ◯ A ◯ B ◯ C

8. When during editing you are looking for a movement with a prominent screen-left direction, you should consult the (A) *vectors column in the VR log* (B) *vector notation on the timeline* (C) *storyboard.*

    8 ◯ A ◯ B ◯ C

9. Nonlinear systems (A) *allow* (B) *do not allow* random access to the source material and use (C) *videotape* (D) *disk-based storage systems.* **(Fill in two bubbles.)**

    9 ◯ A ◯ B
      ◯ C ◯ D

10. When importing uncompressed high-definition video, your files will (A) *take longer and require more storage space* (B) *require more storage space but take less time* (C) *require about the same time and storage space as compressed video.*

    10 ◯ A ◯ B ◯ C

PAGE TOTAL [   ]

11. Audio/video capture from a camcorder to a hard drive is normally done via (A) *digital interface* (B) *S-video cable* (C) *coaxial cable.*

11 (A) (B) (C)

12. When you want the time code to indicate the correct elapsed clock time even for a long running time, you should record the shots in (A) *drop frame mode* (B) *non–drop frame mode* (C) *PAL time code.*

12 (A) (B) (C)

13. The three major components of a nonlinear editing system are (A) *source media, computer, editing software* (B) *server, software, camcorder* (C) *source media, editing software, digitizer.*

13 (A) (B) (C)

14. A VR log must include the (A) *exact shot designation* (B) *in and out time code numbers* (C) *approximate length of each clip.*

14 (A) (B) (C)

15. Audio transcriptions are important especially when editing (A) *a fully scripted 30-second commercial* (B) *an interview* (C) *a fully scripted drama.*

15 (A) (B) (C)

PAGE TOTAL

16. Fill in the bubbles whose letters correspond with the appropriate features of the generic nonlinear editing interface as shown in the following figure.

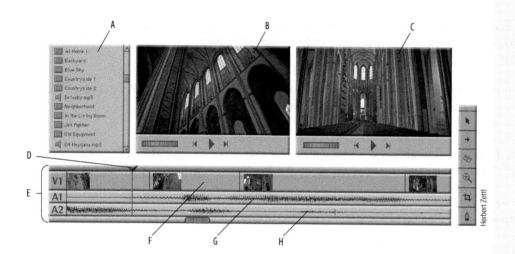

Herbert Zettl

a. audio track 2

16a ⭘ ⭘ ⭘ ⭘
   A B C D
⭘ ⭘ ⭘ ⭘
E F G H

b. source monitor

16b ⭘ ⭘ ⭘ ⭘
   A B C D
⭘ ⭘ ⭘ ⭘
E F G H

c. audio track 1

16c ⭘ ⭘ ⭘ ⭘
   A B C D
⭘ ⭘ ⭘ ⭘
E F G H

d. video track

16d ⭘ ⭘ ⭘ ⭘
   A B C D
⭘ ⭘ ⭘ ⭘
E F G H

e. timeline

16e ⭘ ⭘ ⭘ ⭘
   A B C D
⭘ ⭘ ⭘ ⭘
E F G H

P A G E
T O T A L

f. record monitor

g. project panel

h. playhead and scrubber bar

REVIEW QUIZ

*Mark the following statements as true or false by filling in the bubbles in the **T** (for true) or **F** (for false) column.*

		T	F
1.	Raw footage has a high compression ratio.	1 ○	○
2.	*Off-line editing* means to initially import the source material into the NLE system at a relatively high compression.	2 ○	○
3.	The AB-roll concept does not work for nonlinear editing.	3 ○	○
4.	A split edit refers to editing audio portions separately from video.	4 ○	○
5.	In nonlinear editing, the video and audio frames are not actually sequenced but told by the NLE in what order to play back.	5 ○	○
6.	The vectors column in a good VR log can show the screen direction of somebody's gaze or movement.	6 ○	○
7.	*Shot* and *take* mean the same thing.	7 ○	○
8.	The less video and audio files are compressed, the more storage space they require.	8 ○	○
9.	In a window dub, each frame has a unique address.	9 ○	○
10.	A codec is relatively unimportant in the capturing phase.	10 ○	○
11.	When traffic sounds precede the shot of the street, it represents a split edit.	11 ○	○
12.	Transitions and effects must be integrated during the editing of clips because they cannot be added after the rough-cut.	12 ○	○
13.	All NLE systems have at least two audio tracks.	13 ○	○
14.	A cutaway shot can help solve vector problems.	14 ○	○
15.	Time code can be added to the source footage in postproduction.	15 ○	○
16.	*Capture* means to import clips on the storage system of the editing computer.	16 ○	○
17.	The principle of postproduction editing is file management.	17 ○	○
18.	Replacing a brief clip sequence in the middle of an edited project is quite difficult and time consuming in nonlinear editing.	18 ○	○

SECTION TOTAL [   ]

PROBLEM-SOLVING APPLICATIONS

1. The news producer tells you, the editor, not to bother with an audio transcription of the recent two-hour interview with the mayor because he needs only about 20 seconds of a few memorable sound bites. What is your reaction? Why?

2. The novice director warns you, the editor, that the new client is known to change her mind frequently and may require substantive editing changes right in the middle of the show. The director is worried that such major changes may cause serious time delays. What would you tell the director? Be specific.

3. The same director tells you to be sure to capture all source media at the highest resolution even for an off-line rough-cut because "once in the computer, you are stuck with what you imported." What is your reaction? Why?

4. Even with your new postproduction editing system, it is cumbersome to find shots that show the new car model traveling in specific screen directions. The producer suggests that you note the various vectors when logging the source footage. What does she mean? How can doing this help you locate the desired shots?

5. The director is a big fan of nonlinear editing because fixing mistakes in postproduction is "now a snap." What is your reaction? Give specific examples.

6. The producer hands you a number of source media from a nature videographer. The program idea is to match the video of the movement of various wild animals to the tempo and the feel of some classical music pieces. He wants you to especially emphasize and juxtapose shots in which the animals move in opposite directions—much like the music. Which logging element would facilitate this editing job?

19 Editing Functions and Principles

REVIEW OF KEY TERMS

Match each term with its appropriate definition by filling in the corresponding bubble.

(A) cutaway

(B) complexity editing

(C) index vector

(D) jump cut

(E) graphic vector

(F) motion vector

(G) vector

(H) montage

(I) continuity editing

(J) mental map

(K) vector line

1. a shot that is inserted to facilitate continuity

1	A ○	B ○	C ○	D ○
	E ○	F ○	G ○	H ○
	I ○	J ○	K ○	

2. a vector created by someone looking or something pointing unquestionably in a specific direction

2	A ○	B ○	C ○	D ○
	E ○	F ○	G ○	H ○
	I ○	J ○	K ○	

3. the preservation of visual continuity from shot to shot

3	A ○	B ○	C ○	D ○
	E ○	F ○	G ○	H ○
	I ○	J ○	K ○	

PAGE
TOTAL [   ]

(A) cutaway	(E) graphic vector	(I) continuity editing
(B) complexity editing	(F) motion vector	(J) mental map
(C) index vector	(G) vector	(K) vector line
(D) jump cut	(H) montage	

4. the juxtaposition of two or more shots to generate a third overall idea, which may not be contained in any one

4 Ⓐ Ⓑ Ⓒ Ⓓ
  Ⓔ Ⓕ Ⓖ Ⓗ
  Ⓘ Ⓙ Ⓚ

5. a perceivable force with a direction and a magnitude

5 Ⓐ Ⓑ Ⓒ Ⓓ
  Ⓔ Ⓕ Ⓖ Ⓗ
  Ⓘ Ⓙ Ⓚ

6. the juxtaposition of shots that helps intensify the screen event

6 Ⓐ Ⓑ Ⓒ Ⓓ
  Ⓔ Ⓕ Ⓖ Ⓗ
  Ⓘ Ⓙ Ⓚ

7. juxtaposing shots that violate the established continuity

7 Ⓐ Ⓑ Ⓒ Ⓓ
  Ⓔ Ⓕ Ⓖ Ⓗ
  Ⓘ Ⓙ Ⓚ

8. established by two people facing each other or through a prominent movement in a specific direction

8 Ⓐ Ⓑ Ⓒ Ⓓ
  Ⓔ Ⓕ Ⓖ Ⓗ
  Ⓘ Ⓙ Ⓚ

PAGE
TOTAL

9. virtual image of where things are or are supposed to be in on- and off-screen space

9 ◯ ◯ ◯ ◯
   A B C D
   ◯ ◯ ◯ ◯
   E F G H
   ◯ ◯ ◯
   I J K

10. created by an object actually moving or perceived as moving on-screen

10 ◯ ◯ ◯ ◯
    A B C D
    ◯ ◯ ◯ ◯
    E F G H
    ◯ ◯ ◯
    I J K

11. created by lines or by stationary elements in such a way as to suggest a line

11 ◯ ◯ ◯ ◯
    A B C D
    ◯ ◯ ◯ ◯
    E F G H
    ◯ ◯ ◯
    I J K

PAGE TOTAL [ ]

SECTION TOTAL [ ]

REVIEW OF CONTINUITY-EDITING PRINCIPLES

Select the correct answers and fill in the bubbles with the corresponding letters.

1. From the screen images below, select the sequence pair you would get when cutting from camera 1 to camera 2 as shown in the diagrams of the camera positions on the facing page.

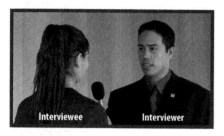

A

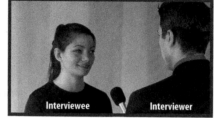

B

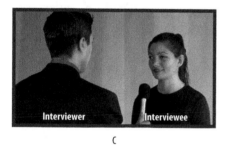

C

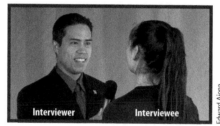

D

Also indicate whether continuity is (E) *good* or (F) *poor*.

a. first camera setup *(Fill in three bubbles.)*

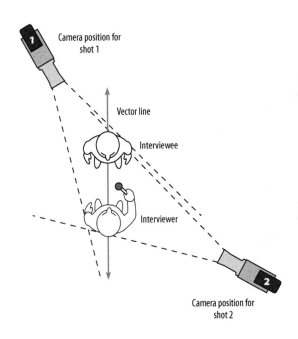

Camera position for shot 1

Vector line

Interviewee

Interviewer

Camera position for shot 2

b. second camera setup *(Fill in three bubbles.)*

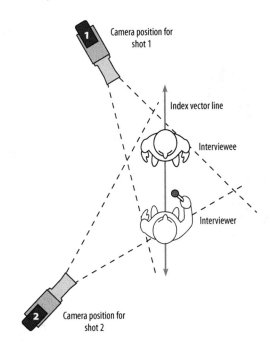

Camera position for shot 1

Index vector line

Interviewee

Interviewer

Camera position for shot 2

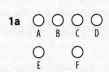

1a ○ ○ ○ ○
    A B C D
    ○   ○
    E   F

1b ○ ○ ○ ○
    A B C D
    ○   ○
    E   F

PAGE TOTAL [ ]

© 2015 Cengage Learning

2. You are given a storyboard to assist you in your single-camera EFP of a conversation between a man and a woman (see the following figure). For each storyboard pair, indicate whether the shots (A) *can* (B) *cannot* be edited together, assuming normal continuity-editing principles.

a.

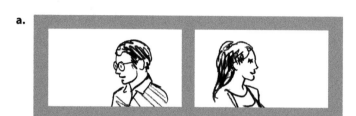

2a   ◯   ◯
      A   B

b.

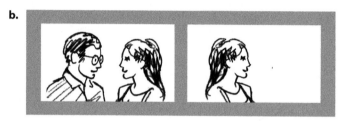

2b   ◯   ◯
      A   B

c.

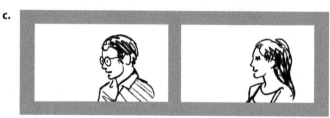

2c   ◯   ◯
      A   B

d.

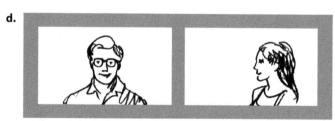

2d   ◯   ◯
      A   B

e.

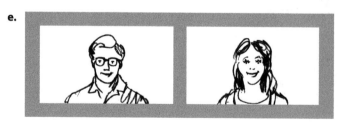

2e   ◯   ◯
      A   B

PAGE
TOTAL   [   ]

3. In the following four diagrams, select the camera that is in the *wrong* place for proper continuity editing and fill in the corresponding bubble.

a. cutting from two-shots of piano player and singer to CUs

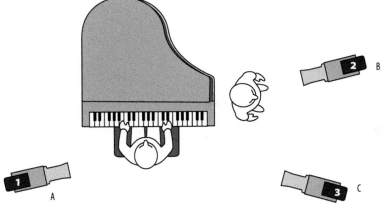

b. cutting from camera 2 to a different point of view of the university president and her husband during a reception

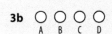

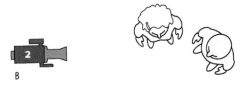

PAGE
TOTAL

c. editing a dramatic car chase

3c ○   ○   ○
    A   B   C

A

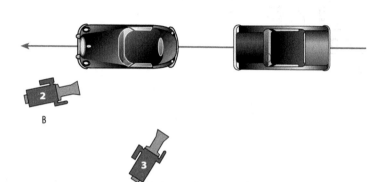

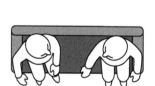
B

C

d. cutting between two people during a conversation

3d ○ ○ ○ ○
    A B C D

D

A

B

C

PAGE
TOTAL

4. In the following diagram of a simple interview, select the two cameras that will facilitate optimal cross-shooting and fill in the bubbles with the corresponding letters.

A

Host

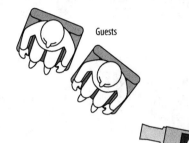

Guests

B

D

C

© 2015 Cengage Learning

5. From the nine frame grabs of source clips below, select four shots to tell the story of a woman getting into her car and driving off. Fill in the bubbles with the letters of the shots you selected in the order you would edit them together.

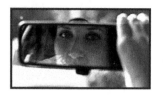

A

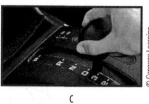

B

C

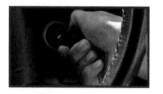

D

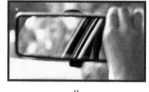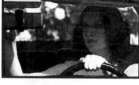

E

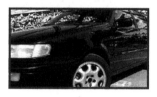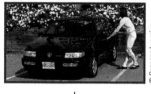

F

G

H

I

a. shot 1

b. shot 2

c. shot 3

d. shot 4

5a ○ ○ ○ ○ ○
    A B C D E
  ○ ○ ○ ○
  F G H I

5b ○ ○ ○ ○ ○
    A B C D E
  ○ ○ ○ ○
  F G H I

5c ○ ○ ○ ○ ○
    A B C D E
  ○ ○ ○ ○
  F G H I

5d ○ ○ ○ ○ ○
    A B C D E
  ○ ○ ○ ○
  F G H I

PAGE
TOTAL

6. For each of the following shot sequences, fill in the appropriate bubbles to indicate whether the sequence (A) *maintains* or (B) *disturbs* the mental map. If the mental map is disturbed, also indicate whether the major reason is a (C) *position switch* or (D) *vector problem*. (***Multiple answers are possible.***)

a.

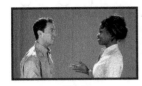 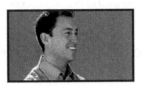 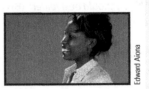

Shot 1   Shot 2   Shot 3

6a   ○ A   ○ B   ○ C   ○ D

b.

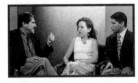 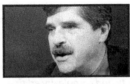 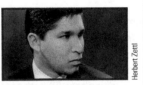

Shot 1   Shot 2   Shot 3

6b   ○ A   ○ B   ○ C   ○ D

c.

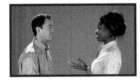 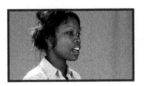 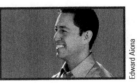

Shot 1   Shot 2   Shot 3

6c   ○ A   ○ B   ○ C   ○ D

d.

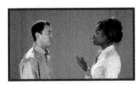 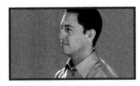 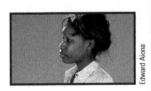

Shot 1   Shot 2   Shot 3

6d   ○ A   ○ B   ○ C   ○ D

P A G E
T O T A L

S E C T I O N
T O T A L

REVIEW OF COMPLEXITY-EDITING PINCIPLES

Select the correct answers and fill in the bubbles with the corresponding letters.

1. In complexity editing, DVE (A) *should be avoided* (B) *can be used to intensify a scene* (C) *can be used to clarify a scene.*

2. A filmic shorthand in which a rhythmic series of seemingly unrelated shots generates new meaning is called a (A) *montage* (B) *clip* (C) *sequence.*

3. Complexity editing (A) *can occasionally break with continuity principles* (B) *must adhere to continuity principles* (C) *does not consider continuity principles.*

4. In complexity editing, a jump cut (A) *clearly signals an editing mistake* (B) *should never be used* (C) *can be used as an intensifier.*

5. A series of quick cuts between camera 1 and camera 2 in the figure below would be appropriate in (A) *continuity editing only* (B) *both continuity and complexity editing* (C) *instantaneous editing.*

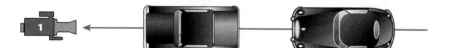

6. The simultaneity of several separate events can best be shown with (A) *multiple screens* (B) *flashbacks* (C) *flashforwards.*

	A	B	C
1	○	○	○
2	○	○	○
3	○	○	○
4	○	○	○
5	○	○	○
6	○	○	○

PAGE TOTAL [   ]

7. In the context of continuity editing, cutting from shot 1 to shot 2 as shown below is (A) *acceptable* (B) *unacceptable* because (C) *the edit would cause a jump cut* (D) *the motion vectors are continuing.*

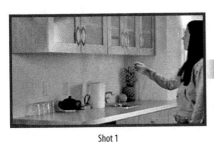 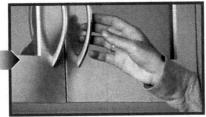

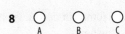

| Shot 1 | Shot 2 |

8. Assuming that you intend to construct a montage of a car fleeing the police, quick cuts among all four cameras shown in the figure below would be appropriate (A) *under no circumstances* (B) *in continuity editing* (C) *in complexity editing.*

8 ○ A ○ B ○ C

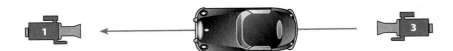

PAGE
TOTAL

SECTION
TOTAL

REVIEW QUIZ

*Mark the following statements as true or false by filling in the bubbles in the **T** (for true) or **F** (for false) column.*

		T	F
1.	Ethical considerations are the purview of the director and have no place in the busy news-editing room.	1 ○	○
2.	If the move is properly motivated, the vector line can be crossed in continuity editing.	2 ○	○
3.	A shrinking circle wipe is an especially effective way to close a documentary on a flood disaster.	3 ○	○
4.	A jump cut may be used effectively in complexity editing.	4 ○	○
5.	A jump cut occurs when the subject has moved his head even slightly from one shot to the next.	5 ○	○
6.	When cutting from an MS to a CU of somebody sitting down, continuity is best preserved by cutting after the person is seated.	6 ○	○
7.	A cutaway can be any shot so long as it does not constitute a vector.	7 ○	○
8.	Sound is an important factor in maintaining continuity.	8 ○	○
9.	Two of the major editing functions are to shorten and to combine.	9 ○	○
10.	So long as we can recognize a person, it does not matter even in continuity editing that she appears on screen-left in one shot and on screen-right in the next.	10 ○	○
11.	A mental map helps viewers organize on- and off-screen space.	11 ○	○
12.	The 2D vector line extends from the camera to the horizon.	12 ○	○
13.	A blurred still shot of a car represents a motion vector.	13 ○	○
14.	Editing must always be done in the context of ethics—the principles of right conduct.	14 ○	○
15.	Somebody pointing at an object constitutes an index vector.	15 ○	○
16.	*Subject continuity* means that we can recognize a person from one shot to the next.	16 ○	○

SECTION
TOTAL [ ]

PROBLEM-SOLVING APPLICATIONS

1. Select a scene from any type of television show or film that demonstrates complexity editing. Be specific.

2. Use a camcorder and ad-lib a scene in which your crossing the line contributes to an intensified experience.

3. The staging for a presidential debate shows two candidates side by side, facing the audience; a moderator is in the middle, facing the candidates, with his back to the audience. The primary cameras are located in the audience, pointing at the stage. One camera is backstage, exactly opposite the moderator. It is to get three-shots in which we see the backs of the candidates and the moderator as he addresses the candidates. Assuming that the objective is seamless continuity, do you have any concerns about this setup? Be specific.

4. The producer tells you not to worry about using a stock shot of videographers for a necessary cutaway in the editing of a news conference. What is your reaction? Be specific.

Scale: ¼" = 1'

Property List

Scale: ¼" = 1'

Property List

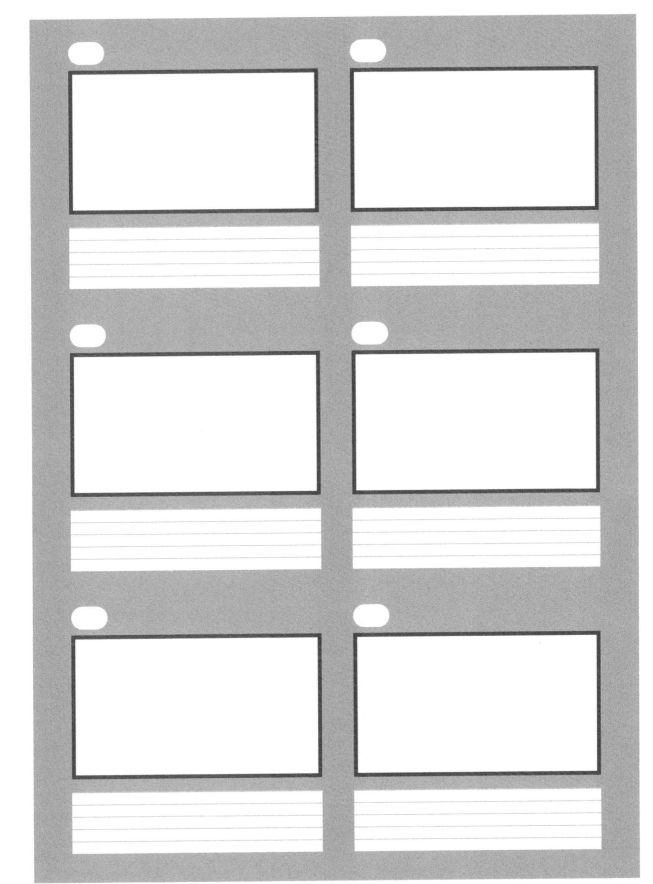

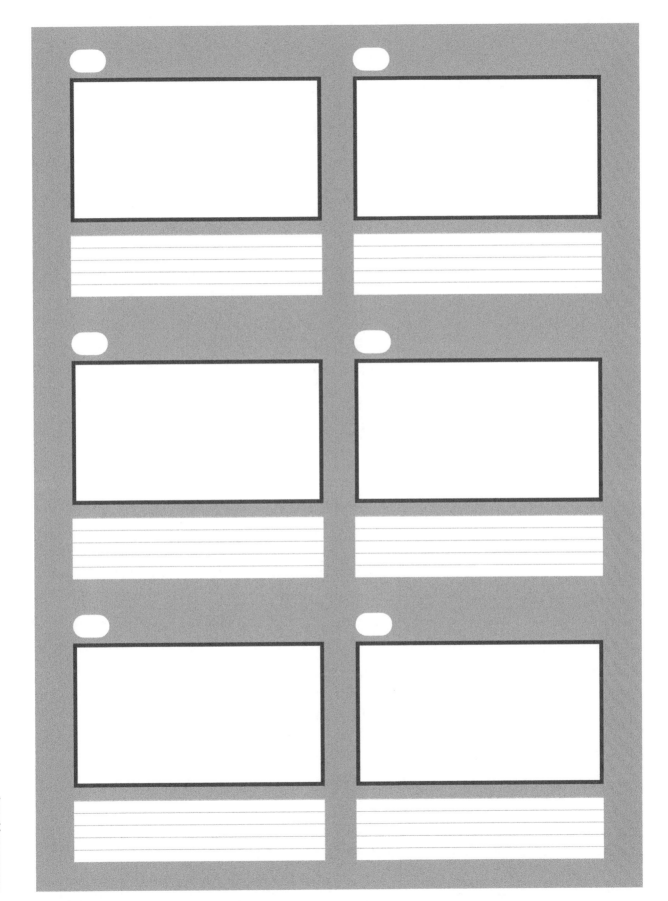